Table of Contents

CHAPTER SIX: ON LOVE

CHAPTER SEVEN: ON SERVANTHOOD

CHAPTER EIGHT: ON DISCOURAGEMENT

CHAPTER NINE: ON FINISHING WELL

EPILOGUE

Meet *Me* in the
LIBRARY

Readings from Eight Writers Who Shaped My Life

Selected and Introduced by

CHARLES R. SWINDOLL

MEET ME IN THE LIBRARY
Readings from Eight Writers Who Shaped My Life
Selected and Introduced by Charles R. Swindoll

Charles R. Swindoll has devoted his life to the clear, practical teaching and application of God's Word and His grace. A pastor at heart, Chuck has served as senior pastor to congregations in Texas, Massachusetts, and California. He currently pastors Stonebriar Community Church in Frisco, Texas, but Chuck's listening audience extends far beyond a local church body. As a leading program in Christian broadcasting, *Insight for Living* airs in major Christian radio markets around the world, reaching people groups in languages they can understand. Chuck's extensive writing ministry has also served the body of Christ worldwide and his leadership as president and now chancellor of Dallas Theological Seminary has helped prepare and equip a new generation for ministry. Chuck and Cynthia, his partner in life and ministry, have four grown children and ten grandchildren.

We would like to acknowledge the following publishers and individuals for permission to reprint the following material.

"Destination: Shandia" from *Through Gates of Splendor* by Elisabeth Elliot. Copyright © 1957, renewed 1985 by Elisabeth Elliot, published by Tyndale House Publishers. Used by permission.

"God Incomprehensible" from *The Knowledge of the Holy; The Attributes of God: Their Meaning in the Christian Life* by A.W. Tozer. Copyright © 1961 by Aiden Wilson Tozer. Reprinted by permission of HarperCollins Publishers.

"Praise God for the Furnace" from *The Root of the Righteous* by A.W. Tozer. Copyright © 1955 by A.W. Tozer, renewed 1983 by Lowell Tozer. Used by permission.

"In the Secret of His Presence" from *The Secret of Guidance* by F.B. Meyer, originally published in 1896.

"That Your Joy May Be Full" from *Abide in Christ* by Andrew Murray, originally published in 1895.

The Mark of the Christian by Francis Schaeffer. Copyright © 1970 by L'Abri Fellowship. Used by permission of InterVarsity Press, PO Box 1400, Downers Grove, IL 60515. www.ivpress.com.

"The Master's Master Principle" from *Spiritual Leadership* by J. Oswald Chambers. Copyright © 1967, 1980, 1994, 2007 by The Moody Bible Institute of Chicago. Used by permission.

"The Minister's Fainting Fits" from *Lectures to My Students* by Charles Haddon Spurgeon, originally published in 1875.

"Discipleship: 'How Will You Compete with Horses?'" from *A Long Obedience in the Same Direction* by Eugene Peterson. Copyright © 1980 by Inter-Varsity Christian Fellowship. Used by permission of InterVarsity Press, PO Box 1400, Downers Grove, IL 60515. www.ivpress.com.

Published By:
IFL Publishing House
A Division of Insight for Living
Post Office Box 251007
Plano, Texas 75025-1007

Editor in Chief: Cynthia Swindoll, President, Insight for Living
Executive Vice President: Wayne Stiles, Th.M., D.Min., Dallas Theological Seminary
General Editor: Barb Peil, M.A., Christian Education, Dallas Theological Seminary
Theological Editor: John Adair, Th.M., Ph.D., Dallas Theological Seminary
Content Editor: Amy L. Snedaker, B.A., English, Rhodes College
Copy Editors: Jim Craft, M.A., English, Mississippi College
        Kathryn Merritt, M.A., English, Hardin-Simmons University
Project Coordinator/Editor, Creative Ministries: Melanie Munnell, M.A., Humanities,
        The University of Texas at Dallas
Project Coordinator, Publishing and Web: Sarah Magnoni, A.A.S., University of Wisconsin
Proofreader: Paula McCoy, B.A., English, Texas A&M University-Commerce
Designer: Kari Pratt, B.A., Commercial Art, Southwestern Oklahoma State University
Production Artist: Nancy Gustine, B.F.A, Advertising Art, University of North Texas

ISBN: 978-0-57972-891-5
Printed in the United States of America

A Letter from Chuck

On a lonely Greyhound bus in January 1958, a young Marine slumped in his seat with his head down. His heart ached for the wife he'd left behind and feared for the place he was headed. In his hands, he held Elisabeth Elliot's book, *Through Gates of Splendor*. As he turned the pages, his life was turned around forever . . .

That was me.

I had no idea what God had in store for me when I boarded that bus. It turned out to be one of my life's defining moments . . . and it came to me through a book. God used Elisabeth Elliot's volume to rearrange my attitude, my thinking . . . my entire future. You'll read about it in the pages that follow.

God has used other books and their significant messages in my life. I'd like to introduce you to a few. I want to encourage you with the truths I've learned from them and to tell you a bit about their authors. My hope is that you will be strengthened and challenged by these grand messengers that have pointed the way for me.

At a time when the publishing industry pushes out thousands of new books in print each year and even more than that electronically, I want to share with you selections from nine works that endure—works that have inspired me to reach higher and further. You'll see they touch on various aspects of the Christian life: suffering, joy, prayer, and servanthood, to name a few. Across time and generations, these great books carry the truths of God and the thoughts and feelings of the human spirit. They are worth passing on, and each one should be read in the next generation and beyond.

What books would make your list? Consider the authors who speak into your life — the ones whose writings have defined your life in some way. This volume you now hold is my short list. I could easily add a dozen more books for each topic mentioned, but this is a good place to start.

So, let's do just that.

Chuck Swindoll

Charles R. Swindoll

Meet *Me* in the
LIBRARY

Chapter One

ON PURSUING ONE'S CALLING

My Defining Moment

by Charles R. Swindoll

I remember it like it was yesterday: it was 1958. The rain splashed against the window of the Greyhound bus as it drove south on California's Interstate 5 from Pasadena to Camp Pendleton. It was one of the most vulnerable times in my life.

The Crisis

A few months earlier, I had joined the Marine Corps . . . not the Navy, because they promoted, "Join the Navy and see the world." I was not interested in seeing the world. I wanted to stay close to home with my new wife, to finish my military obligation, and to get back on stream in a career that was waiting for me at a large industry in Houston.

I had made two mistakes. First, I had talked to the Marine Corps recruiting officer. And second, I had believed him. He had promised me that I would never have to go overseas . . . in fact, there was no chance whatsoever that I would have to worry about leaving the States, my wife, and our families during my tour of duty. I remember his words, "No chance you'll go abroad, young man."

Cynthia and I had settled down in a quaint, lovely apartment in Daly City, California, for my first, and what I hoped would be my only, place of military duty in the Corps. One normal afternoon, I received a letter from Washington. I thought it was the standard form letter, so I didn't bother to open it until I was in my car, waiting outside the place where Cynthia worked. With a view of San Francisco Bay, I cut open this piece of mail and sat in shock at its announcement. The letter was orders from my commanding officer via President Eisenhower, stating that my "military occupational specialty" (MOS) was needed on Okinawa. I had no idea where that even was. But just the word *Okinawa* burned itself into the pit of my stomach.

I wanted two things. I wanted the letter to be a mistake, and I wanted Okinawa to be a little town in south Texas. I later learned *Okinawa* was affectionately known as "The Rock," just like the prison Alcatraz that I could see out in the bay in front of me as I opened those orders. I'll never forget the overwhelming disillusionment that swept over me.

Those emotions only intensified during the next month, especially when I said good-bye to my young bride and traveled south to Camp Pendleton, where I waited in a staging regiment for my upcoming overseas deployment.

My entire life had turned on a dime in the direction of the other side of the world. Though I knew the Lord, I rehearsed all the ways He was letting me down. Candidly, I felt ripped off. Confused. Resentful. Disillusioned about life . . . about God. I had never felt more alone than in those days of getting ready to make a seventeen-day voyage across the Pacific Ocean on a troopship, first to Japan, and then to a little island in the slender Ryukyuan chain of islands, southeast of Japan.

The Book

I had liberty on the weekend before I was to ship out, so I took a bus from Pendleton to Pasadena, where my older brother, Orville, was living at the time.

I was in a foul mood the whole weekend. My anger was so close to the surface that I was close to crying or cursing. As I was getting ready to leave late Sunday evening, I was near tears as I said to Orville, "I've about had it with this whole thing." I grunted and groaned as I was shoving things in my bag to leave.

He said, "I want you to take this book with you." It was *Through Gates of Splendor*, a new book written by a missionary wife whose husband, Jim Elliot, had been martyred just two years earlier in Ecuador. Jim, along with four other godly young men, had attempted to reach the Auca Indians, known today as the Huaorani.

I said back to Orville, "I don't want to read that."

He said, "I really want you to read it."

I threw it back across the table, grumbling, "I *said* I don't want to read it."

He walked around the table, took me by the arm, and said, "If you begin to read this book, you'll never be able to put it down. Take it! Read it."

And so on a rainy Sunday night as the big Greyhound bus rumbled south toward Camp Pendleton, I flipped on the light over my seat and opened the book. Immediately, God began to speak. I devoured that book, page after page, picture after picture. I read names I had never heard before . . . Jim Elliot. Nate Saint. Roger Youderian. Pete Fleming. Ed McCully. Those men, being dead, still spoke. Some of the pictures were hard to look at — their bodies floating in the Curaray River, one with a broken spear still sticking out of his hip. I started trying to imagine such a brutal, tragic death.

I read all night. Mind you, I didn't *want* to read it, but I couldn't stop. I read in the men's room since it was the only place on base where the light stayed on 24/7. I read all 256 pages, finishing it about 10 a.m. the next morning. I was enraptured by the true story of bravery, commitment, and devotion.

Elisabeth Elliot described the remarkable account of her husband, Jim, and these four other fine men of God who, though young, had amazing vision, mixed with faith and abandonment. I could hardly pronounce all their names, but I understood that kind of lifestyle . . . and I was rebuked by their choices. They all had said no to all the other things life offered them and a firm yes to God. They had packed up and moved to Ecuador with a passion to reach the souls of those "savages." And on January 8, 1956 — almost to the day two years before — all five gave up their lives.

It was the perfect time for me to read their story, just before going overseas. It peeled the scales from my eyes. It got my focus off myself.

For the first time, I began to accept the fact that my transfer overseas just might have been arranged by God (!) and that God's world program somehow might include me, of all people. Without God's initial and forceful plan to get me to leave the States, I would never have caught His vision for the entire world to know Christ. And I mean, *never*.

It was a wrenching experience, but God got my attention. No one could have been more stubborn than I. No one could possibly have following Christ further on the back list of his or her mind than I did during that time in my life. There I was, a thin, young Marine about to be pushed eight thousand miles away from home, not realizing this was God's way of showing me His plan for my life — a plan so different than what I was gripping white-knuckled, unwilling to release.

Reading It for the Second Time

I read the book for the second time on the troopship a few days later in early January 1958. Only then did I see Jim Elliot's words, "He is no fool who gives what he cannot keep to gain what he cannot lose." [1] I had missed it the first time through. I'll never forget how those sixteen words pierced my heart. It just about did me in.

It dawned on me, at last, what a fool I had been, how selfishly my life had been spent. I was appropriately rebuked. This experience became the making of me as a man and the turning point in my spiritual walk.

Up until that night, I was interested in saving my life, not losing it — getting my way, not giving it up. I was a Christian, but I had no plans for God's interference in my life. You may relate perfectly to where I was. You may read these words right now — and understand what I'm saying — and yet continue to live your life light-years removed from this truth. If this description matches you too, then I fear for you. Stay on this track, and you'll miss what life is all about. Strangely, life — real life — is about death. Life is about being separated from what we want and being connected to what God wants.

I arrived in Okinawa a different man, ready for God to break through my life in the most unexpected ways.

During the months that followed, I witnessed with my own eyes what life was like outside the United States. I got involved with The Navigators, which led me into evangelism, street meetings, Bible studies, and various projects designed to present the claims of Christ to the lost. Those many months I spent on that Southeast Asian island further expanded my horizons.

My experience, coupled with the reading of several missions books, created within me a desire to minister on a broader base than simply the familiar United States. I longed to reach beyond the comfortable realm of the expected — the only world I had understood up until then.

And the Rest Is History

After sixteen months away, I returned to the U.S. and to my lovely wife, Cynthia, with a completely transformed perspective on life and ministry. Of course, she had been tracking right along with me through long letters back and forth that expressed our new-found passion for ministry. God had aligned her heart alongside mine. In the fall of 1959, I enrolled in Dallas Theological Seminary. Wow — what a transformation from the disillusioned, angry, young man who had left the States a lifetime before!

Little did Cynthia or I ever think that the turning point in our lives and ministry — my deployment to Okinawa way back in the late 1950s — would one day result in our having a part in extending the light of hope to people around the world. But that's how God works, isn't it? He, being sovereign, takes life's disappointments, which seem at the moment to be nothing more than a mysterious series of events, a hopeless knot of tangled threads, and He weaves them into the starting point of a great tapestry of opportunities we would never have expected and otherwise never experienced.

The testimony of five men who gave their lives to reach a never-before-known people group turned this young Marine's life around. I never knew these men personally. Nevertheless, they became models of vision and courage that stirred faith in me. To this day, I pause and think of them.

I was recently reminded of what their testimony means to me when I was sitting alone late one evening, reading a Christian periodical commemorating the fiftieth anniversary of their deaths. I closed the magazine at the end of that particular article and turned off the lights. I looked out the window, up into the sky, and I remembered.

The images from the book came back like a flash. Five bodies floating face-down in the Curaray River. Ah, the American press covered the story with a barrage of constant sarcasm. *"In vain! In vain! What a waste! What a waste!"* But who knows how many thousands said yes to Christ because of the witness and martyrdom of Jim Elliot and his fellow soldiers of the cross?

I was one of the thousands.

In my own way, I was as distant from God as those "savages" who had never heard of Christ. In God's infinite plan, He chose to take the lives of those five men so the Aucas might be reached and people like me might give full attention to the ministry to which God called us.

God will be glorified . . . whether by life or by death.

Destination: Shandia

from *Through Gates of Splendor*

by Elisabeth Elliot

After eighteen days at sea Jim Elliot and Pete Fleming arrived in Guayaquil, Ecuador. "About half-way up the Guayas River," wrote Pete, "I finally comprehended that this, *this* was Ecuador. I felt a tingling sensation for the first time. Jim and I sang quietly, 'Faith of our Fathers,' as the boat pulled into the harbor:

> *"'Faith of our Fathers, holy faith*
> *We will be true to thee till death.'"*

Leaving the ship, the two young men made their way through the stacks of baggage out into the hot sunlight on the Malacon, the parkway beside the Guayas River. The tide was coming in, and out in the center of the current, great masses of water hyacinths rode swiftly upriver. A gleaming white fruit ship stood at anchor, and beside it crowded the barges and long slim dugout canoes of banana vendors. A ferry was disgorging its sweating, shouting multitudes, with their straw suitcases, cloth bundles, chickens, and baskets. Jim and Pete stopped to watch the faces until the crowd dissipated in all directions; then they turned and crossed the street. Portals over the sidewalk shaded them from the tropical sun, and they gazed at the store windows with their astonishingly heterogeneous displays: sweaters and typewriters, frying pans and automobile tires, fake shrunken heads from the Jivaro Indians, and Camay soap. In one side street, cocoa beans were spread out like a nubbly red-brown carpet to dry in the sun. Businessmen, dressed in crisp white suits and Panama hats, were coming out of the buildings for their two-hour lunch break. Cadillacs and donkeys, nudging each other for the right of way, epitomized this land of contrasts.

With a growing population of over three hundred thousand, Guayaquil is the country's largest and most modern city, with wide streets and imposing office buildings. The streets are crowded, as owners, managers, and clerks from the various importing and exporting firms bustle about their business. Guayaquil is the banana capital of the world, and also from here, since World War II, more than three million bags of coffee, some seventy million pounds of cocoa, and more than three hundred million pounds of rice have annually been loaded for the export market. An air of prosperity prevails, production is constantly rising, and, this port city serves as the country's trade barometer.

Pete and Jim spent their first night in a third-class hotel. Heat, mosquitoes, the occasional bray of a burro, and the Latin rhythm of a dance band nearby made the night a memorable one. The next day they took a plane to Quito, traveling up over the western cordillera of the Andes, crossing a 13,000-foot pass, and landing in the capital of Ecuador. Quito is 9,300 feet above sea level, and to the west rises the volcanic mountain Pichincha.

Here was a new opportunity to "live to the hilt." This old-world city, with its adobe houses, high mud walls, cobblestone streets, ornate churches, with its red geraniums and eucalyptus trees, was to be their home for the next six months. For before they could get to the Oriente—the eastern jungle area of Ecuador, goal of their tireless preparation and planning—there remained this last requirement, the learning of Spanish, the national language of Ecuador.

They signed up for Spanish lessons with a *señorita* who expected nothing short of perfection, and they also engaged a room in the home of an Ecuadorian doctor who had five children. Here was an unparalleled opportunity for practice. They were forced to speak Spanish, and the children were quite uninhibited in pointing out the mistakes and peculiarities of their guests.

"Señor Jaime," said little Moquetin, a bright-eyed imp of six, "why is it that your face is always red?" Jim countered, "Why is it that *your* face is always brown?" "Because it is much prettier that way," was the unexpected reply.

"Language is a tyranny of frustration," Pete once said. But learn it they must. During those months of study Pete wrote in his diary: "I am longing now to reach the Aucas if God gives me the honor of proclaiming the Name among them. . . . I would gladly give my life for that tribe if only to see an assembly of those proud, clever, smart people gathering around a table to honor the Son—gladly, gladly, gladly! What more could be given to a life?

"These almost six months have been crammed full of goodness and God has given us special privileges by way of having no set responsibilities, of giving us the money and the freedom to live with a national family and undoubtedly we have learned things that will stand us in good stead all our missionary lives. And it has been a terrific boon; praying together and seeing God give us faith, getting more and more from the Spanish Bible, gradually finding Spanish easier and getting useful phrases fixed in my mind so I didn't have to think out every one. It has all been good and we have learned things: how to cope with situations and how to keep our mouths shut on some subjects, how to get along with the nationals, what their perspective on missionaries is. . . . God is going to give us Spanish by one means or another, and Quichua as well."

Finally the day came when Jim and Pete were to leave Quito. They saw their gear thrown up on top of a fat, ungainly vehicle that served as a bus. An American truck bed had been surmounted by an amazing superstructure that protruded on both sides, accommodating perhaps thirty or more passengers inside, and as many as dared cling on the outside. Squeezing themselves and their cameras, hallmark of the missionary as well as of the tourist, in among the other riders, they each found a seat—a board perhaps ten inches wide, with as much room again for the legs, between it and the next seat. They were fortunate indeed to be in a bus with an aisle, for in some vehicles passengers cheerfully clamber over the backs of the seats to their places. And they were able to sit up straight and still see out of the low windows. To have one's knees close to one's chin is not the most comfortable position, but then, they could take turns sitting by the aisle to stretch their legs.

"*Vamos!*" called the driver. Jim and Pete rejoiced that the bus was going to start on schedule. But no such luck this time — for this is the land of *mañana*. Everywhere there are unexplained delays, and perhaps most trying thing of all to an outsider is the fact that no one seems to be the least interested in giving an explanation. No questions are asked. Silence. In this case, the delay lasted only ten minutes or so; and, without warning, the driver gunned his motor and the bus lurched to a start.

Leaving the city, the bus climbed up over the paramo, where a cold drizzle added to the bleakness of great stretches of brown grass. An occasional Indian galloped by on horseback, red wool poncho flying in the strong wind. A woman dressed in a heavy wool skirt and embroidered blouse passed at a dog trot, the usual gait of the Indian of the high Andes. Her baby, dressed exactly as she was, complete with fedora, joggled in a cloth on her back. The mother's hands moved nimbly, spinning wool on a spindle.

At 12,000 feet the men could see the small grass huts of the highland Quichuas. They eke out a living herding cattle and sheep, growing potatoes and certain grains. This scene was soon replaced by the arid territory surrounding Ambato, the city of the earthquake of 1949, and the "gateway to the Oriente." Here the bus stopped, and was immediately besieged by women with their trays of fried pork, meat pies, glasses of fruit drink, or slices of pineapple piled into an enamel basin. Each called her wares in a peculiar singsong.

The trip was resumed once more, with the bus climbing up between lofty, snow-clad peaks, then tipping forward to swoop down in dizzy, hairpin turns into the vast gorge cut by the Pastaza River through the eastern cordillera of the Andes, past the cone-shaped Tungurahua, an extinct volcano. With startling suddenness the desert of the western slope and the high mountain pass were replaced by lush greenness on the breathtaking eastern descent. Purple orchids nodded out over the road as the bus swayed and jerked along the narrow shelf of road, a precipice on the right, a steep wall of rock shouldering up on the left. Toward late afternoon the bus rounded another curve, and the Pastaza spread itself out before them, flowing in broad ribbons over black beaches. This was the western extreme of the mighty Amazon basin, which terminates three thousand miles to the east, as the river empties into the Atlantic Ocean. Another little town or two, and Shell Mera was reached. A former base of the Shell Oil Company for prospecting operations in the area, it is now an unpretentious huddle of dilapidated wooden buildings: houses, a hotel, and stores on one side of the road, and an army base and mission-sponsored Bible school on the other.

The Ecuador base of the Missionary Aviation Fellowship was at the southern end of town. Here Jim and Pete met Dr. Tidmarsh, the missionary with whom they had corresponded before coming to Ecuador. And with him they were soon flying north from Shell Mera, over the green sea of jungle, following the Ansuc River toward the Atun Yaku, headwaters of the Napo.

They were headed for Shandia, the Quichua mission station which Dr. Tidmarsh had had to abandon because of his wife's health. They planned to reopen the station, Dr. Tidmarsh staying till they could get established. Shandia did not at this time have an airstrip, so the three flew to another station nearby. Here they landed and set out on foot through the jungle. It was late in the afternoon when they started, and knowing that it was normally a three-hour hike, they raced against the sudden tropical twilight. Slipping on grassy roots, stumbling and struggling through deep mud at times, they pressed eagerly on to the place that would be their home for months to come. They were full of anticipation for what lay ahead, but at the same time they drank in the beauties of the great Amazon rain forest through which they passed.

It was virgin jungle. Trees with great buttress-shaped roots grew to tremendous heights, often with no branches except at the top. Under these umbrellas an incredible variety of flora thrives. It was often impossible for Jim and Pete to distinguish the leaves which belong properly to the trees, for the huge tangle of lianas, air plants, and fungus that sponge a living from them. Orchids everywhere lent their soft colors to the living green. Fungus grew in vivid colors and bizarre shapes—vermilion, shaped like the ruffle on a lady's dress; turquoise, shaped like a shell, half hidden under a rotten log.

Just as the moon rose over the forest, the three men burst into the clearing that was Shandia.

"Indians immediately gathered around," wrote Pete, "and I remembered a couple of faces from Tidmarsh's pictures, and felt a kind of pride in remembering. My first thought was, 'Yes, I can love these people.' The ink-colored designs on the women's faces interested me and the pitiful drape of the faded blue skirts. Lots of children were about, smiling shyly. Babies sucked on big, tremulous breasts, and the young, eager faces of boys looked up at us. Heard Tidmarsh's first conversation in Quichua; wondered how I would ever learn it."

At the same time Jim wrote: "We have arrived at the destination decided on in 1950. My joy is full. Oh how blind it would have been to reject the leading of these days. How it has changed the course of life for me and added such a host of joys!"

At the far end of the clearing stood the small thatched house in which Dr. Tidmarsh had lived. It was walled with split bamboo, floored with boards, and set on posts to insure circulation of air and to give protection from both the damp ground and the invasion of insects.

"At my first glance the house looked spacious and comfortable," Pete wrote in his diary, "and I thought how easily Olive and I could live in such a set-up, feeling joy in the knowledge and anticipation. Afterwards we got cleaned up a bit, washed our muddy feet in the ice-cold Napo, took a look around, and settled down to a meal of rice soup, plantain, manioc, and rice, with coffee. Now by the light of the kerosene lamp I am writing on the dining room table . . . tired but full of thankfulness to the Father, who leads on. In reality, this is not an end but a beginning."

Elisabeth Elliot Gren

(1926–)

For the first forty years of her life, Elizabeth Elliot, known among friends as Betty, was driven by her passion for foreign missions. While preparing for the missions field and attending Wheaton College, she met her future husband, Jim Elliot; they later married in Ecuador. Amazingly, Betty persisted in ministering to the Aucas (now called the Huaorani) for two years after the tribe killed Jim and four other missionaries in 1956. After returning to the United States, Betty continued her ministry through writing and speaking. Her insights into developing an active faith in God, even through paths of suffering, were developed in more than twenty books. Betty and her husband, Lars, live in New England.

Chapter Two

ON INTIMACY
WITH GOD

Knowing the Unknowable

by Charles R. Swindoll

Lost in silent solitude, I often have been impressed anew with the vast handiwork of our incomprehensible God.

The psalmist was correct: the heavens *do* indeed tell of the glory of God . . . their expanse *does* indeed declare the work of His hands (Psalm 19:1). When you mix that unfathomable fact with the incredible reality that He cares for each one of us right down to the last, tiniest detail, the psalmist is, again, correct: such knowledge is beyond me . . . I cannot even imagine it (139:6).

I find God's incomprehensibility absolutely refreshing. It's delightful to be reminded anew that "our God is in the heavens" and "He does whatever He pleases" (115:3). He doesn't ask permission. He doesn't bother to explain. He simply does "whatever He pleases," thank you. After all, He is the Lord . . . the Maker of heaven and earth, the sovereign God of all the universe.

We need that reminder, we who are tempted to think we're capable of calling the shots. How many times must our incomprehensible God tell us, "My ways are past finding out," before we begin to believe it? Since the Son of God found it necessary at the crossroads of His earthly existence to pray, "Not as I will, but as You will" (Matthew 26:39), we would be wise to use the same eight words often. Like . . . every day!

The more I ponder the world around us and the universe above us—be it the starry skies or the stormy seas or the majestic mountains—the more I want to pause, stand still, and let the wonder in. That's when we see God as who He should be to us—namely *God incomprehensible*. Holy? Of course. Powerful? Yes, no question. Compassionate? Always. Righteous and just? Gracious, loving, self-sufficient, sovereign? All the above, certainly.

But He is more . . . so much more.

More than we can grasp. More than we can measure or predict. More than the brightest among us can even *imagine*.

And what are the benefits of such realization? We no longer reduce Him to manageable terms. We're no longer tempted to manipulate Him or His Word. We don't have to explain Him and His will or defend Him and His ways.

Our God is incomprehensible . . . yet, we long to know more about Him. The words of A. W. Tozer from his book *The Knowledge of the Holy* have provided me with a place to begin. How does one embark upon a discovery of who God is? Humbly. And with awe.

Tozer's prayer below expresses it beautifully. You can continue following his thoughts as you read the selection that comes after.

> Lord, how great is our dilemma! In Thy Presence silence best becomes us, but love inflames our hearts and constrains us to speak.
>
> Were we to hold our peace, the stones would cry out; yet if we speak, what shall we say? Teach us to know that we cannot know, for the things of God knoweth no man, but the Spirit of God. Let faith support us where reason fails, and we shall think because we believe, not in order that we may believe.
>
> In Jesus' name. *Amen.*[1]

God Incomprehensible

from *The Knowledge of the Holy*

by A. W. Tozer

The child, the philosopher, and the religionist have all one question: "What is God like?"

This book is an attempt to answer that question. Yet at the outset I must acknowledge that it cannot be answered except to say that God is not like anything; that is, He is not *exactly* like anything or anybody.

We learn by using what we already know as a bridge over which we pass to the unknown. It is not possible for the mind to crash suddenly past the familiar into the totally unfamiliar. Even the most vigorous and daring mind is unable to create something out of nothing by a spontaneous act of imagination. Those strange beings that populate the world of mythology and superstition are not pure creations of fancy. The imagination created them by taking the ordinary inhabitants of earth and air and sea and extending their familiar forms beyond their normal boundaries, or by mixing the forms of two or more so as to produce something new. However beautiful or grotesque these may be, their prototypes can always be identified. They are like something we already know.

The effort of inspired men to express the ineffable has placed a great strain upon both thought and language in the Holy Scriptures. These being often a revelation of a world above nature, and the minds for which they were written being a *part* of nature, the writers are compelled to use a great many "like" words to make themselves understood.

When the Spirit would acquaint us with something that lies beyond the field of our knowledge, He tells us that *this* thing is *like* something we already know, but He is always careful to phrase His description so as to save us from slavish literalism. For example, when the prophet Ezekiel saw heaven opened and beheld visions of God, he found himself looking at that which he had no language to describe. What he was seeing was wholly different from anything he had ever known before, so he fell back upon the language of resemblance. "As for the likeness of the living creatures, their appearance was like burning coals of fire."

The nearer he approaches to the burning throne the less sure his words become: "And above the firmament that was over their heads was the likeness of a throne, as the appearance of a sapphire stone: and upon the likeness of the throne was the likeness as the appearance of a man above upon it. And I saw as the colour of amber, as the appearance of fire round about within it. . . . This was the appearance of the likeness of the glory of the Lord."

Strange as this language is, it still does not create the impression of unreality. One gathers that the whole scene is very real but entirely alien to anything men know on earth. So, in order to convey an idea of what he sees, the prophet must employ such words as "likeness," "appearance," "as it were," and "the likeness of the appearance." Even the throne becomes "the appearance of a throne" and He that sits upon it, though like a man, is so *unlike* one that He can be described only as "the likeness of the appearance of a man."

When the Scripture states that man was made in the image of God, we dare not add to that statement an idea from our own head and make it mean "in the *exact* image." To do so is to make man a replica of God, and that is to lose the unicity of God and end with no God at all. It is to break down the wall, infinitely high, that separates

That-which-is-God from that-which-is-not-God. To think of creature and Creator as alike in essential being is to rob God of most of His attributes and reduce Him to the status of a creature. It is, for instance, to rob Him of His infinitude: there cannot be two unlimited substances in the universe. It is to take away His sovereignty: there cannot be two absolutely free beings in the universe, for sooner or later two completely free wills must collide. These attributes, to mention no more, require that there be but one to whom they belong.

When we try to imagine what God is like we must of necessity use that-which-is-not-God as the raw material for our minds to work on; hence whatever we visualize God to be, He is not, for we have constructed our image out of that which He has made and what He has made is not God. If we insist upon trying to imagine Him, we end with an idol, made not with hands but with thoughts; and an idol of the mind is as offensive to God as an idol of the hand.

"The intellect knoweth that it is ignorant of Thee," said Nicholas of Cusa, "because it knoweth Thou canst not be known, unless the unknowable could be known, and the invisible beheld, and the inaccessible attained."[1]

"If anyone should set forth any concept by which Thou canst be conceived," says Nicholas again, "I know that that concept is not a concept of Thee, for every concept is ended in the wall of Paradise. . . . So too, if any were to tell of the understanding of Thee, wishing to supply a means whereby Thou mightest be understood, this man is yet far from Thee . . . forasmuch as Thou art absolute above all the concepts which any man can frame."[2]

Left to ourselves we tend immediately to reduce God to manageable terms. We want to get Him where we can use Him, or at least know where He is when we need Him. We want a God we can in some measure control. We need the feeling of security that comes

from knowing what God is like, and what He is like is of course
a composite of all the religious pictures we have seen, all the best
people we have known or heard about, and all the sublime ideas we
have entertained.

If all this sounds strange to modern ears, it is only because we
have for a full half century taken God for granted. The glory of God
has not been revealed to this generation of men. The God of contemporary Christianity is only slightly superior to the gods of Greece and
Rome, if indeed He is not actually inferior to them in that He is weak
and helpless while they at least had power.

If what we conceive God to be He is not, how then shall we
think of Him? If He is indeed incomprehensible, as the Creed
declares Him to be, and unapproachable, as Paul says He is, how
can we Christians satisfy our longing after Him? The hopeful words,
"Acquaint now thyself with him, and be at peace," still stand after the
passing of the centuries; but how shall we acquaint ourselves with
One who eludes all the straining efforts of mind and heart? And how
shall we be held accountable to know what cannot be known?

"Canst thou by searching find out God?" asks Zophar the
Naamathite; "canst thou find out the Almighty unto perfection? It
is high as heaven; what canst thou do? deeper than hell; what canst
thou know?" "Neither knoweth any man the Father, save the Son,"
said our Lord, "and he to whomsoever the Son will reveal him." The
Gospel according to John reveals the helplessness of the human mind
before the great Mystery which is God, and Paul in I Corinthians
teaches that God can be known only as the Holy Spirit performs in
the seeking heart an act of self-disclosure.

The yearning to know What cannot be known, to comprehend
the Incomprehensible, to touch and taste the Unapproachable, arises
from the image of God in the nature of man. Deep calleth unto deep,

and though polluted and landlocked by the mighty disaster theologians call the Fall, the soul senses its origin and longs to return to its Source. How can this be realized?

The answer of the Bible is simply "through Jesus Christ our Lord." In Christ and by Christ, God effects complete self-disclosure, although He shows Himself not to reason but to faith and love. Faith is an organ of knowledge, and love an organ of experience. God came to us in the incarnation; in atonement He reconciled us to Himself, and by faith and love we enter and lay hold on Him.

"Verily God is of infinite greatness," says Christ's enraptured troubadour, Richard Rolle; "more than we can think; . . . unknowable by created things; and can never be comprehended by us as He is in Himself. But even here and now, whenever the heart begins to burn with a desire for God, she is made able to receive the uncreated light and, inspired and fulfilled by the gifts of the Holy Ghost, she tastes the joys of heaven. She transcends all visible things and is raised to the sweetness of eternal life. . . . Herein truly is perfect love; when all the intent of the mind, all the secret working of the heart, is lifted up into the love of God."[3]

That God can be known by the soul in tender personal experience while remaining infinitely aloof from the curious eyes of reason constitutes a paradox best described as

> Darkness to the intellect
> But sunshine to the heart.
>
> *Frederick W. Faber*

The author of the celebrated little work *The Cloud of Unknowing* develops this thesis throughout his book. In approaching God, he says, the seeker discovers that the divine Being dwells in obscurity, hidden behind a cloud of unknowing; nevertheless he should not be discouraged but set his will with a naked intent unto God. This cloud is between the seeker and God so that he may never see God clearly by the light of understanding nor feel Him in the emotions. But by the mercy of God faith can break through into His Presence if the seeker but believe the Word and press on.[4]

Michael de Molinos, the Spanish saint, taught the same thing. In his *Spiritual Guide* he says that God will take the soul by the hand and lead her through the way of pure faith, "and causing the understanding to leave behind all considerations and reasonings He draws her forward. . . . Thus He causes her by means of a simple and obscure knowledge of faith to aspire only to her Bridegroom upon the wings of love."[5]

For these and similar teachings Molinos was condemned as a heretic by the Inquisition and sentenced to life imprisonment. He soon died in prison, but the truth he taught can never die. Speaking of the Christian soul he says: "Let her suppose that all the whole world and the most refined conceptions of the wisest intellects can tell her nothing, and that the goodness and beauty of her Beloved infinitely surpass all their knowledge, being persuaded that all creatures are too rude to inform her and to conduct her to the true knowledge of God. . . . She ought then to go forward with her love, leaving all her understanding behind. Let her love God as He is in Himself, and not as her imagination says He is, and pictures Him."[6]

"What is God like?" If by that question we mean "What is God like *in Himself*?" there is no answer. If we mean "What has God disclosed *about Himself* that the reverent reason can comprehend?" there is, I believe, an answer both full and satisfying. For while the name of God is secret and His essential nature incomprehensible,

He in condescending love revelation declared certain things to be true of Himself. These we call His attributes.

> Sovereign Father, heavenly King,
> Thee we now presume to sing;
> Glad thine attributes confess,
> Glorious all, and numberless.

> *Charles Wesley*

A. W. (Aiden Wilson) Tozer

(1897–1963)

For generations, God has used the pen of A. W. Tozer to stir the hearts of believers in Jesus Christ. For most of Tozer's ministry years, he was pastor of Southside Alliance Church in Chicago and concurrently editor of The Alliance Witness. *His work behind both the pen and the pulpit prompted most of his books, essays, and devotionals widely known today, especially the classics,* The Pursuit of God *and* The Knowledge of the Holy.

Chapter Three

ON TRIALS
AND TESTING

The Essential Season of Suffering

by Charles R. Swindoll

If there is anything that draws us close together as humans, it is this: we all hurt. Some more intensely, more deeply, more profoundly than others, but we all know pain. Though we often view pain as an enemy, it is an essential part of God's inexplicable curriculum that leads to obedience.

It's a painful truth: suffering is essential if we hope to become effective for God. God has at His disposal whatever He wishes to bring into our lives. And to the surprise of those who've not stopped to think about it, among those things are suffering and pain. God wants us to be growing, becoming whole, mature, strong, and enduring. He wants us wise and deep, not silly and shallow.

A. W. Tozer was right when he said, "It is doubtful whether God can bless a man greatly until He has hurt him deeply." [1] C. S. Lewis put it this way, "God whispers to us in our pleasures, speaks in our conscience, but shouts in our pains: it is His megaphone to rouse a deaf world." [2]

Solomon, in his journal named Ecclesiastes, wrote:

> Consider the work of God,
> For who is able to straighten what He has bent?
> In the day of prosperity be happy,
> But in the day of adversity consider —
> God has made the one as well as the other.
> (7:13–14)

Psalm 119 echoes this same thought:

Before I was afflicted I went astray,
But now I keep Your word. (119:67)

It is good for me that I was afflicted,
That I may learn Your statutes. (119:71)

I know, O Lord, that Your judgments are righteous,
And that in faithfulness You have afflicted me.
(119:75)

If you have reached the place in your Christian life where you are beyond the message of today's superficial theology, you are prepared for this truth.

Suffering softens our spirits and makes us sensitive to God's voice. He doesn't leave us alone in our pain. In the stark reality of whatever may be the affliction, God quiets us and calms us and reminds us again that everything that occurs reaches us after being filtered through His hand and permitted for His purposes and glory.

Although this journey along the avenue of affliction is unpleasant and unappealing, it is both inevitable and essential. No one in God's family can remain a stranger to pain and suffering. Working through the hurt is essential if we hope to become effective for God.

That's the heart of A. W. Tozer's message in the following essay, "Praise God for the Furnace," from his work *The Root of the Righteous*. Read it thoughtfully, prayerfully. Don't rush through it. Take time to ponder God's hand in your life.

Praise God for the Furnace

from *The Root of the Righteous*

by A. W. Tozer

It was the enraptured [Samuel] Rutherford who could shout in the midst of serious and painful trials, "Praise God for the hammer, the file and the furnace."

The hammer is a useful tool, but the nail, if it had feeling and intelligence, could present another side of the story. For the nail knows the hammer only as an opponent, a brutal, merciless enemy who lives to pound it into submission, to beat it down out of sight and clinch it into place. That is the nail's view of the hammer, and it is accurate except for one thing: The nail forgets that both it and the hammer are servants of the same workman. Let the nail but remember that the hammer is held by the workman and all resentment toward it will disappear. The carpenter decides whose head shall be beaten next and what hammer shall be used in the beating. That is his sovereign right. When the nail has surrendered to the will of the workman and has gotten a little glimpse of his benign plans for its future it will yield to the hammer without complaint.

The file is more painful still, for its business is to bite into the soft metal, scraping and eating away the edges till it has shaped the metal to its will. Yet the file has, in truth, no real will in the matter, but serves another master as the metal also does. It is the master and not the file that decides how much shall be eaten away, what shape the metal shall take, and how long the painful filing shall continue. Let the metal accept the will of the master and it will not try to dictate when or how it shall be filed.

As for the furnace, it is the worst of all. Ruthless and savage, it leaps at every combustible thing that enters it and never relaxes its fury till it has reduced it all to shapeless ashes. All that refuses to burn is melted to a mass of helpless matter, without will or purpose of its own. When everything is melted that will melt and all is burned that will burn, then and not till then the furnace calms down and rests from its destructive fury.

With all this known to him, how could Rutherford find it in his heart to praise God for the hammer, the file and the furnace? The answer is simply that he loved the Master of the hammer, he adored the Workman who wielded the file, he worshiped the Lord who heated the furnace for the everlasting blessing of His children. He had felt the hammer till its rough beatings no longer hurt; he had endured the file till he had come actually to enjoy its bitings; he had walked with God in the furnace so long that it had become as his natural habitat. That does not overstate the facts. His letters reveal as much.

Such doctrine as this does not find much sympathy among Christians in these soft and carnal days. We tend to think of Christianity as a painless system by which we can escape the penalty of past sins and attain to heaven at last. The flaming desire to be rid of every unholy thing and to put on the likeness of Christ at any cost is not often found among us. We expect to enter the everlasting kingdom of our Father and to sit down around the table with sages, saints and martyrs; and through the grace of God, maybe we shall; yes, maybe we shall. But for the most of us it could prove at first an embarrassing experience. Ours might be the silence of the untried soldier in the presence of the battle-hardened heroes who have fought the fight and won the victory and who have scars to prove that they were present when the battle was joined.

The devil, things and people being what they are, it is necessary for God to use the hammer, the file and the furnace in His holy work of preparing a saint for true sainthood. It is doubtful whether God can bless a man greatly until He has hurt him deeply.

Without doubt we of this generation have become too soft to scale great spiritual heights. Salvation has come to mean deliverance from unpleasant things. Our hymns and sermons create for us a religion of consolation and pleasantness. We overlook the place of the thorns, the cross and the blood. We ignore the function of the hammer and the file.

Strange as it may sound, it is yet true that much of the suffering we are called upon to endure on the highway of holiness is an inward suffering for which scarcely an external cause can be found. For our journey is an inward journey, and our real foes are invisible to the eyes of men. Attacks of darkness, of despondency, of acute self-depreciation may be endured without any change in our outward circumstances. Only the enemy and God and the hard-pressed Christian know what has taken place. The inward suffering has been great and a mighty work of purification has been accomplished, but the heart knoweth its own sorrow and no one else can share it. God has cleansed His child in the only way He can, circumstances being what they are. Thank God for the furnace.

A. W. (Aiden Wilson) Tozer

(1897–1963)

For generations, God has used the pen of A. W. Tozer to stir the hearts of believers in Jesus Christ. For most of Tozer's ministry years, he was pastor of Southside Alliance Church in Chicago and concurrently editor of The Alliance Witness. *His work behind both the pen and the pulpit prompted most of his books, essays, and devotionals widely known today, especially the classics,* The Pursuit of God *and* The Knowledge of the Holy.

Chapter Four

ON PRAYER

A Tree Fell in Fullerton

by Charles R. Swindoll

A number of years ago, not far from the house where my wife and I lived for twenty-three years in Fullerton, California, a large section of a tree fell to the ground. The grand tree was one of the landmarks that gave our neighborhood its dignity and character plus a touch of charm.

Nobody saw it happen . . . but within minutes, several of us had gathered to grieve the loss. Those once sturdy branches full of leaves spread awkwardly across the sidewalk. As I stood there staring in disbelief, the thought struck me, *This didn't just happen . . . it's been in process for a long time.*

No tree suddenly breaks apart and plunges to the ground.

We tree-lovers had no way of knowing until it was too late. Once we were able to see beneath the thick bark and inside the tree through the break, it was obvious that some kind of killer disease had been at work. Slowly, silently, secretly, deep within the core of that tall and handsome timber, an erosion had been underway—an erosion which could not remain hidden forever.

Within a couple of hours, the city workers arrived in their orange trucks filled with heavy equipment; they had everything cut up, swept up, and whisked away in no time. Cleaning up after a fallen tree is a rather quick and efficient matter.

Not so with a fallen life.

Unlike trees, people don't grow up all alone or exist in a world of stoic and sterile independence. We mingle and merge into one another's lives. Neither our laughter nor our tears remain aloof. Our roots get intertwined, the fruit we bear gets mutually enjoyed, and because we care for one another, we provide strength for each other on hot, barren days and in windy seasons. At times however, out of respect for privacy, we give each other space, trusting one another in realms too personal to share with everyone.

But therein lies the rub. It is in this unmentionable realm, this altogether personal region of intimacy, that trouble begins. It's there where a core disease in the thought-life goes unnoticed and untreated. It's there a tragic inner erosion begins its downward path toward destruction. No one knows that behind our healthy-looking bark, our heart is neither wholesome nor healthy. No one realizes the slow, silent, secret erosion over the years. Then one day—like that leafy giant at the end of my block—a person suddenly plunges to the ground, diseased to the core.

One of my author-mentors is the British pastor, F. B. Meyer. From him, I've learned about the tragic lesson of erosion. I recall that he once wrote: "No man suddenly becomes base." Slowly—almost imperceptibly—things are tolerated that were once rejected. At the outset, it appears harmless. But with it comes a seemingly insignificant wedge—a gap that grows wider as moral erosion joins hands with spiritual decay.

How do we guard ourselves from this secret killer? You'll find part of the answer in the following chapter from F. B. Meyer's book *The Secret of Guidance*, originally published in 1896. Titled "In the Secret of His Presence," this chapter illustrates how spiritual strength comes from deep within—from attending to what's not seen. The answer to that "how" is *prayer*. Make the secret place of fellowship with the Lord your daily destination. And be on your guard—that secret place is the first place compromised when your relationship with God begins to erode. Small wonder we're warned, "Above all else, guard your heart" (Proverbs 4:23 NIV).

Learn to listen to the Spirit's prompting in those private moments of prayer. Hide nothing from Him. He sees your inner thoughts and motivations through and through. Prayer is the only way the subtle, slow slip of erosion can be prevented or stopped before it's too late.

In the Secret of His Presence

from *The Secret of Guidance*

by F. B. Meyer

In one sense God is always near us. He is not an absentee, needing to be brought down from the heavens or up from the deep. He is near at hand. His Being pervades all being. Every world that floats like an island in the ocean of space is filled with signs of His presence, just as the home of your friend is littered with many evidences of his residence, by which you know that he lives there, though you have not seen his face. Every crocus pushing through the dark mold; every firefly in the forest; every bird that springs up from its nest before your feet; everything that is — *all* are as full of God's presence as the bush that burned with His fire, before which Moses bared his feet in acknowledgment that God was there.

But we do not always realize it. We often pass hours, and days, and weeks. We sometimes engage in seasons of prayer, we go to and fro from His house, where the ladder of communication rests; and still He is a shadow, a name, a tradition, a dream of days gone by.

> Oh that I knew where I might find him! that I might come even to his seat! . . . Behold, I go forward, but he is not there; and backward, but I cannot perceive him: On the left hand, where he doth work, but I cannot behold him: he hideth himself on the right hand, that I cannot see him. (Job 23:3, 8–9)

How different is this failure to realize the presence of God to the blessed experience of His nearness realized by some!

Brother Lawrence, the simple cook, for more than sixty years never lost the sense of the presence of God, but was as conscious of it while performing the duties of his humble office as when partaking of the Holy Supper.

John Howe, on the blank page of his Bible, made this record in Latin: "This very morning I awoke out of a most ravishing and delightful dream, when a wonderful and copious stream of celestial rays, from the lofty throne of the Divine Majesty, seemed to dart into my open and expanded breast. I have often since reflected on that very signal pledge of special Divine favor, and have with repeated fresh pleasure tasted the delights thereof."

Are not these experiences, so blessed and inspiring, similar to that of the author of the longest, and in some respects, the sublimest Psalm in the Psalter? He had been beating out the golden ore of thought through the successive paragraphs of marvelous power and beauty, when suddenly he seems to have become conscious that He of whom he had been speaking had drawn near, and was bending over him. The sense of the presence of God was borne in upon this inner consciousness. And, lifting up a face on which reverence and ecstasy met and mingled, he cried, "Thou art near, O Lord" (Psalm 119:151).

If only such an experience of the nearness of God were always ours, enfolding us as air or light; if only we could feel, as the great apostle put it on Mars' Hill, that God is not far away but the element in which we have our being, as sea flowers live in deep, still lagoons: then we should understand what David meant when he spoke about dwelling in the house of the Lord all the days of his life, beholding His beauty, inquiring in His temple, and hiding in the secret of His pavilion (Psalm 27:4–5). Then, too, we should acquire the blessed secret of *peace, purity,* and *power.*

In the Secret of His Presence
There Is Peace

"In the world ye shall have tribulation," our Master said, but "in me ye might have peace" (John 16:33). It is said that a certain insect has the power of surrounding itself with a film of air, encompassed in which it drops into the midst of muddy, stagnant pools and remains unhurt. And the believer is also conscious that he is enclosed in the invisible film of the divine presence, as a far-traveled letter in the envelope that protects it from hurt and soil.

"They draw nigh that follow after mischief," but You are nearer than the nearest, and I dwell in the inner ring of Your presence. The mountains round about me are filled with the horses and chariots of Your protection. No weapon that is formed against me can prosper, for it can only reach me through You, and, touching You, it will glance harmlessly aside.

To be in God is to be in a well-fitted house when the storm has slipped from its leash; or in a sanctuary, the doors of which shut out the pursuer.

In the Secret of His Presence
There Is Purity

The mere vision of snow-capped Alps, seen from afar across Lake Geneva, so elevates and transfigures the rapt and wistful soul as to destroy all evil things that would thrust themselves upon the inner life. The presence of a little child, with his guileless purity, has been known to disarm passion, as a beam of light, falling in a reptile-haunted cave, scatters the snakes.

But what shall not Your presence do for me, if I acquire a perpetual sense of it, and live in its secret place? Surely, in the heart of that fire, black cinder though I be, I shall be kept pure, and glowing, and intense!

In the Secret of His Presence
There Is Power

My cry, day and night, is for power—spiritual power. Not the power of intellect, oratory, or human might. These cannot avail to vanquish the serried ranks of evil.

You say truly that it is not by might nor by power. Yet human souls that touch You become magnetized, charged with a spiritual force that the world can neither gainsay nor resist. Oh! let me touch You! Let me dwell in unbroken contact with You, that out of You successive tides of divine energy may pass into and through my emptied and eager spirit, flowing, but never ebbing, and lifting me into a life of blessed ministry, which shall make deserts blossom like the garden of the Lord.

But how shall we get and keep this sense of God's nearness? Must we go back to Bethel, with its pillar of stone where even Jacob said, "Surely the Lord is in this place" (Genesis 28:16)? Ah, we might have stood beside him, with unanointed eye, and seen no ladder, heard no voice; while the patriarch would discover God in the bare moorlands of our lives, trodden by us without reverence or joy.

Must we travel to the mouth of the cave in whose shadow Elijah stood, thrilled by the music of the still small voice, sweeter by contrast with the thunder and the storm? Alas! we might have stood beside him unconscious of that glorious Presence; while Elijah, if living now, would discern it in the whisper of the wind, the babbling of babies, the rhythm of heartbeats.

If we had stationed ourselves in our present state beside the apostle Paul when he was caught into the third heaven, we should probably have seen nothing but a tentmaker's shop, or a dingy room in a hired lodging—we in the dark, while he was in transports; while he would discern, were he to live again, angels on our steamships, visions in our temples, doors opening into heaven amid the tempered glories of our more somber skies.

In point of fact, we carry everywhere our circumference of light or dark. God is as much in the world as He was when Enoch walked with Him and Moses communed with Him face-to-face. He is as willing to be a living, bright, glorious Reality to us as to them. But the fault is with us. Our eyes are unanointed because our hearts are not right. The pure in heart still see God, and to those who love Him, and do His commandments, He still manifests Himself as He does not to the world. Let us cease to blame our times; let us blame ourselves. We are degenerate, not they.

What, then, is that temper of soul that most readily perceives the presence and nearness of God? Let us endeavor to learn the blessed secret of abiding ever in the secret of His presence and of being hidden in His pavilion (Psalm 31:20).

Remember, then, at the outset, that neither you nor any of our race can have that glad consciousness of the presence of God except *through Jesus.* None knows the Father but the Son and those to whom the Son reveals Him (Luke 10:22); and none comes to the Father but by Him (John 14:6). Apart from Jesus the presence of God is an object of terror, from which devils wish to hide themselves and sinners weave aprons or hide among the trees to cover themselves. But in Him all barriers are broken down, all veils rent, all clouds dispersed. The weakest believer may live where Moses sojourned, in the midst of the fire, before whose consuming flames no impurity can stand.

"What part of the Lord's work is most closely connected with this blessed sense of the presence of God?"

It is through the blood of His Cross that sinners are made near. In His death He not only revealed the tender love of God, but He put away our sins and wove for us those garments of stainless beauty in which we are gladly welcomed into the inner presence-chamber of the King. Remember it is said, "I will commune with thee from above the mercyseat" (Exodus 25:22). And it is when you enter into deepest fellowship with Him in His death, and live most constantly in the spirit of His memorial supper, that you shall realize most deeply His nearness. Now, as at Emmaus, He loves to make Himself known in the breaking of bread.

"And is this all? for I have heard this many times, and still fail to live in the secret place as I would."

Exactly so; and therefore, to do for us what no effort of ours could do, our Lord has received of His Father the promise of the Holy Spirit, that He should bring into our hearts the very presence of God. Understand that since you are Christ's, the blessed Comforter is yours. He is within you as He was within your Lord, and in proportion as you live in the Spirit, and walk in the Spirit, and open your entire nature to Him, you will find yourself becoming His Presence-chamber, irradiated with the light of His glory. And as you realize that He is in you, you will realize that you are ever in Him. Thus the beloved apostle wrote, "Hereby know we that we dwell in him, and he in us, because he hath given us of his Spirit" (1 John 4:13).

"All this I know, and yet I fail to realize this marvelous fact of the indwelling of the Spirit in me; how then can I ever realize my indwelling in Him?"

It is because your life is so hurried. You do not take time enough for meditation and prayer. The Spirit of God within you and the Presence of God without you cannot be discerned while the senses are occupied with pleasure, or the pulse beats quickly, or the brain is filled with the tread of many hurrying thoughts. It is when water stands that it becomes clear and reveals the pebbly beach below. Be still, and know that God is within you and around you. In the hush of the soul the unseen becomes visible and the eternal real. The eye dazzled by the sun cannot detect the beauties of its pavilion till it has had time to rid itself of the glare. Let no day pass without its season of silent waiting before God.

"Are there any other conditions that I should fulfill, so that I may abide in the secret of His presence?"

Be pure in heart. Every permitted sin encrusts the windows of the soul with thicker layers of grime, obscuring the vision of God. But every victory over impurity and selfishness clears the spiritual vision, and there fall from the eyes, as it had been, scales. In the power of the Holy Spirit deny self, give no quarter to sin, resist the devil, and you shall see God.

The unholy soul could not see God even though it were set down in the midst of heaven. But holy souls see God amid the ordinary commonplaces of earth and find everywhere an open vision. Such could not be nearer God though they stood by the sea of glass. Their only advantage there would be that the veil of their mortal and sinful natures having been rent, the vision would be more direct and perfect.

Keep His commandments. Let there be not one jot or tittle unrecognized and unkept. "He that hath my commandments, and keepeth them, he it is that loveth me: and he that loveth me shall be loved of My Father, and I will love him, and will manifest myself to him" (John 14:21). Moses the faithful servant, was also the prophet, and he spoke with God face to face as a man speaks with his friend.

Continue in the spirit of prayer. Sometimes the vision will tarry to test the earnestness and steadfastness of your desire. At other times it will come as the dawn steals over the sky, and, before you are aware, you will find yourself conscious that He is near. He was even accustomed to glide, unheralded, into the midst of His disciples through unopened doors. "Thy footsteps are not known" (Psalm 77:19).

At such times we may truly say with St. Bernard: "He entered not by the eyes, for His presence was not marked by color; nor by the ears, for there was no sound; nor by the breath, for He mingled not with the air; nor by the touch, for He was impalpable. You ask, then, how I knew that He was present. Because He was a quickening power. As soon as He entered, He awoke my slumbering soul. He moved and pierced my heart, which before was strange, stony, hard and sick, so that my soul could bless the Lord, and all that is within me praised His Holy Name."

Cultivate the habit of speaking aloud to God. Not perhaps always, because our desires are often too sacred or deep to be put into words. But it is well to acquire the habit of speaking to God as to a present friend while sitting in the house or walking by the way. Seek the habit of talking things over with God — letters, your plans, your hopes, your mistakes, your sorrows and sins. Things look very different when brought into the calm light of His presence. One cannot talk long with God aloud without feeling that He is near.

Meditate much upon the Word. This is the garden where the Lord God walks, the temple where He dwells, the presence-chamber where He holds court, and it is found by those who seek Him. It is through the word that we feed upon the Word. And He said, "He that eateth my flesh, and drinketh my blood, dwelleth in me, and I in him" (John 6:56).

Be diligent in Christian work. The place of prayer is indeed the place of His manifested presence, but that presence would fade from it were we to linger there after the bell of duty had rung for us below. We shall ever meet it as we go about our necessary work: "Thou meetest him that . . . worketh righteousness" (Isaiah 64:5). As we go forth to our daily tasks the angel of His presence comes to greet us and turns to go at our side. "Go ye," said the Master; "Lo, I am with you always" (Matthew 28:19–20). Not only in temple courts, or in sequestered glens, or in sickrooms, but in the round of daily duty, in the common places of life, on the dead levels of existence, we may be ever in the secret of His presence, and shall be able to say with Elijah before Ahab, and with Gabriel to Zacharias, "I stand in the presence of God" (see 1 Kings 17:1; Luke 1:19).

Cultivate the habit of recognizing the presence of God. "Blessed is the man whom thou choosest, and causest to approach unto thee, that he may dwell in thy courts" (Psalm 65:4). There is no life like this. To feel that God is with us; that He never leads us through a place too narrow for Him to pass as well; that we can never be lonely again, never for a single moment; that we are beset by Him behind and before, and covered by His hand; that He could not be nearer to us, even if we were in heaven itself. To have Him as Friend, and Referee, and Counselor, and Guide. To realize that there is never to be a Jericho in our lives without the presence of the Captain of the Lord's host, with those invisible but mighty legions, before whose charge all walls must fall down. What wonder that the saints of old waxed valiant in fight as they heard Him say, "I will be with thee: I will not fail thee, nor forsake thee" (Joshua 1:5).

Begone fear and sorrow and dread of the dark valley! "Thou shalt hide [me] in the secret of thy presence from the pride of man: thou shalt keep [me] secretly in a pavilion from the strife of tongues" (Psalm 31:20).

F. B. (Frederick Brotherton) Meyer

(1847–1929)

Around the turn of the twentieth century, churches and Christian conferences on both sides of the Atlantic were greatly influenced by the pastoral support and preaching of F. B. Meyer. Through his lifelong friendship with evangelist Dwight L. Moody, Meyer toured England and the United States as a sought-after conference circuit speaker. His passionate appeals against prostitution and drunkenness were said to have influenced the closing of hundreds of brothels and bars. Meyer was also a spokesperson for the Keswick Movement, which teaches that followers of Christ can experience daily victory over sin and abundant life through the power of the Holy Spirit.

Chapter Five

ON JOY

The Secret to Joyful Living

by Charles R. Swindoll

Word pictures flowed freely from our Lord's lips. Whether He was teaching or preaching, rebuking or comforting, He often turned to everyday scenes familiar to His hearers.

Pause and consider a few of these pictures. A sower sowing seed. A bride and her groom. A lost coin. A shepherd with his flock. Thorns and thistles. Crumbs falling from the table. Salt and light. A hen gathering her chicks. Lambs in the midst of wolves. There are dozens of them!

But of all the pictures Jesus painted with His words, none is more vivid or more meaningful to me than the vine and the branches. You may remember the scene recorded in the early verses of John 15. The vineyard scene is portrayed with precision. No detail is left to our imaginations. He even provides the interpretation.

He, Himself, is the true vine. The Father is the vinedresser. We believers are the branches. Clearly, the Savior's desire is to underscore one all-important truth: we are to bear fruit. He prunes us, cleans us up, and nurtures us with that one goal in mind.

But, how do we meet that goal? Is fruit-bearing the result of hard work and dedication? No. How about sincerely giving it our best shot or putting together a strategic plan? Again, no. The one and only solution is abiding. Check it out for yourself. Jesus made it painfully obvious that unless we abide in Him (as a branch must continue to abide in a vine), we *cannot* bear fruit. Nothing is accomplished when we go solo. I suggest you read that again.

Jesus's summary statement says it all: "Apart from Me you can do nothing" (John 15:5).

Let that sink in. Think about it: nothing. Zero. How essential, then, that you and I stay attached to, remain in vital union with, our Lord Jesus Christ! For apart from that all-important connection, nothing of value can be produced. What a counter-culture message in our do-it-yourself society!

I've frequently thought of our lives in terms of another word picture: the seasons. Track that idea with me. Every life must go through the blast furnace of barren summers when fruit bearing is rare. Summer is a season of perseverance. How vital it is that we abide in Christ through the heat of life's summers!

Interestingly, summer is followed by autumn, a season of fruitfulness. The soft-falling rain and cooler breezes bring relief and encouragement—a season of rest. And then comes winter when the world rests beneath a blanket of snow.

Abiding fits both those seasons as well. No branch can ever bear fruit without the vine . . . and no branch can ever endure the harsh winds and pruning of autumn or the bitter blast of winter unless its attachment to the vine remains solid and sure. And then, in turn, comes spring, the season of promise, when the same branches that were pruned back to stumps in autumn show new life . . . fresh buds of hope emerging as drab brown turns to bright shades of green. But, as was true in the other seasons, abiding remains the secret. How well Jesus's word picture of the vine fits with that of the seasons . . . the world that surrounds us every day.

Right after giving us such a powerful word picture, Jesus said, "These things I have spoken to you so that My joy may be in you, and that your joy may be made full" (John 15:11). That's the amazing by-product of abiding in the vine: joy! Regardless of the season, a Christian's life should be marked by gratitude and gladness. *Rejoicing always.* Why? As Andrew Murray, the wonderful South African author and pastor, put it, we rejoice always for "the life of unutterable blessedness to which [we] have been redeemed."[1] Sorrows will come, but we have an everlasting hope. And that is reason enough to be glad.

How does it happen season after season? By abiding in Christ. That's the ticket.

Have you found, as I have, that our faithful and gentle God is a Gardener you can trust? He's too kind to be cruel, too good to be unjust. He prunes but never tortures. And how involved He is! In the Father's vineyard, no branch is ignored . . . no weed is neglected . . . no fruit is overlooked. Through it all, He expects only one thing from us — and rightly so: that we abide in Christ. Abiding is everything!

Are you abiding? Is your inner nourishment coming only from Him? Is He your strength, your hope, your purpose for living? Without Him, remember, there is nothing. Nothing of value. Nothing joyful. Nothing lasting. Nothing to be rewarded.

That Your Joy May Be Full

from *Abide in Christ*

by Andrew Murray

"These things have I spoken unto you,

that my joy might abide in you,

and that your joy might be full."

John 15:11

Abiding fully in Christ is a life of exquisite and overflowing happiness. As Christ gets more complete possession of the soul, it enters into the joy of its Lord. His own joy, the joy of heaven, becomes its own, and that in full measure, and as an ever-abiding portion. Just as joy on earth is everywhere connected with the vine and its fruit, so joy is an essential characteristic of the life of the believer who fully abides in Christ, the heavenly Vine.

We all know the value of joy. It alone is the proof that what we have really satisfies the heart. As long as duty, or self-interest, or other motives influence me, men cannot know what the object of my pursuit or possession is really worth to me. But when it gives me joy, and they see me delight in it, they know that to me at least it is a treasure. Hence there is nothing so attractive as joy, no preaching so persuasive as the sight of hearts made glad. Just this makes gladness such a mighty element in the Christian character: there is no proof of the reality of God's love and the blessing He bestows, which men so soon feel the force of, as when the joy of God overcomes all the trials of life. And for the Christian's own welfare, joy is no less indispensable: the joy of the Lord is his strength; confidence, and courage, and patience find their inspiration in joy. With a heart full of joy no work can weary, and no burden can depress; God Himself is strength and song.

Let us hear what the Saviour says of the joy of abiding in Him. He promises us *His own joy*: "My joy." As the whole parable refers to the life His disciples should have in Him when ascended to heaven, the joy is that of His resurrection life. This is clear from those other words of His (John 16:22): "I will see you again, and your heart shall rejoice, and your joy shall no man take from you." It was only with the resurrection and its glory that the power of the never-changing life began, and only in it that the never-ceasing joy could have its rise. With it was fulfilled the word: "Therefore thy God hath anointed thee with the oil of gladness above thy fellows." The day of His crowning was the day of the gladness of His heart. That joy of His was the joy of a work fully and for ever completed, the joy of the Father's bosom regained, and the joy of souls redeemed. These are the elements of His joy; of them the abiding in Him makes us partakers. The believer shares so fully His victory and His perfect redemption, that his faith can without ceasing sing the conqueror's song: "Thanks be to God, who always causeth me to triumph." As the fruit of this, there is the joy of the undisturbed dwelling in the light of the Father's love—not a cloud to intervene if the abiding be unbroken. And then, with this joy in the love of the Father, as a love received, the joy of the love of souls, as love going out and rejoicing over the lost. Abiding in Christ, penetrating into the very depths of His life and heart, seeking for the most perfect oneness, these the three streams of His joy flow into our hearts. Whether we look backward and see the work He has done, or upward and see the reward He has in the Father's love that passeth knowledge, or forward in the continual accessions of joy as sinners are brought home, His joy is ours. With our feet on Calvary, our eyes on the Father's countenance, and our hands helping sinners home, we have His joy as our own.

And then He speaks of this joy as *abiding*—a joy that is never to cease or to be interrupted for a moment: "That my joy might abide in you." "Your joy no man taketh from you." This is what many Christians cannot understand. Their view of the Christian life is that it is a succession of changes, now joy and now sorrow. And they appeal to the experiences of a man like the Apostle Paul, as a proof of how much there may be of weeping, and sorrow, and suffering. They have not noticed how just Paul gives the strongest evidence as to this unceasing joy. He understood the paradox of the Christian life as the combination at one and the same moment of all the bitterness of earth and all the joy of heaven. "As sorrowful, yet *always rejoicing*": these precious golden words teach us how the joy of Christ can overrule the sorrow of the world, can make us sing while we weep, and can maintain in the heart, even when cast down by disappointment or difficulties, a deep consciousness of a joy that is unspeakable and full of glory. There is but one condition: "*I will see you again*, and your heart shall rejoice, and your joy shall no man take from you." The presence of Jesus, distinctly manifested, cannot but give joy. Abiding in Him consciously, how can the soul but rejoice and be glad? Even when weeping for the sins and the souls of others, there is the fountain of gladness springing up in the faith of His power and love to save.

And this His own joy abiding with us, He wants to be *full*. Of the full joy our Saviour spoke thrice on the last night. Once here in the parable of the Vine: "*These things have I spoken* unto you that your joy might be *full*"; and every deeper insight into the wonderful blessedness of being the branch of such a Vine confirms His Word. Then He connects it (John 16:24) with our prayers being answered: "*Ask and ye shall receive*, that your joy may be *full*." To the spiritual mind, answered prayer is not only a means of obtaining certain blessings, but something infinitely higher. It is a token of our fellowship with the Father and the Son in heaven, of their delight in us, and our having been admitted and having had a voice in that wondrous interchange of love in which the Father and the Son hold counsel, and decide the daily guidance of the children on earth. To a soul abiding in Christ, that longs for manifestations of His love, and that understands to take an answer to prayer in its true spiritual value, as a response from the throne to all its utterances of love and trust, the joy which it brings is truly unutterable. The word is found true: "Ask and ye shall receive, and your joy shall be full." And then the Saviour says, in His high-priestly prayer to the Father (John 17:13), "*These things I speak*, that they might have my joy *fulfilled* in themselves." It is the sight of the great High Priest entering the Father's presence for us, ever living to pray and carry on His blessed work in the power of an endless life, that removes every possible cause of fear or doubt, and gives us the assurance and experience of a perfect salvation. Let the believer who seeks, according to the teaching of John 15, to possess the full joy of abiding in Christ, and according to John 16, the full joy of prevailing prayer, press forward to John 17. Let him there listen to those wondrous words of intercession spoken, that his joy might be full. Let him, as he listens to those words, learn the love that even now pleads for him in heaven without ceasing, the glorious objects for which it is pleading, and which through its all-prevailing pleading are hourly being realized, and Christ's joy will be fulfilled in him.

Christ's own joy, abiding joy, fulness of joy—such is the portion of the believer who abides in Christ. Why, O why is it that this joy has so little power to attract? The reason simply is: Men, yea, even God's children, do not believe in it. Instead of the abiding in Christ being looked upon as the happiest life that ever can be led, it is regarded as a life of self-denial and of sadness. They forget that the self-denial and the sadness are owing to the not abiding, and that to those who once yield themselves unreservedly to abide in Christ as a bright and blessed life, their faith comes true—the joy of the Lord is theirs. The difficulties all arise from the want of the full surrender to a full abiding.

Child of God, who seekest to abide in Christ, remember what the Lord says. At the close of the parable of the Vine He adds these precious words: "*These things* have I spoken unto you, that my joy might abide in you, and that your joy might be full." Claim the joy as part of the branch life—not the first or chief part, but as the blessed proof of the sufficiency of Christ to satisfy every need of the soul. Be happy. Cultivate gladness. If there are times when it comes of itself, and the heart feels the unutterable joy of the Saviour's presence, praise God for it, and seek to maintain it. If at other times feelings are dull, and the experience of the joy not such as you could wish it, still praise God *for the life of unutterable blessedness to which you have been redeemed.* In this, too, the word holds good: "According to your faith be it unto you." As you claim all the other gifts in Jesus, ever claim this one too—not for your own sake, but for His and the Father's glory. "*My joy* in you"; "that *my joy* may *abide* in you"; "*my joy fulfilled* in themselves"—these are Jesus' own words. It is impossible to take Him wholly and heartily, and not to get His joy too. Therefore, "Rejoice in the Lord always; and again I say, Rejoice."

Andrew Murray

(1828–1917)

God's Spirit was on the move in South Africa in the 1860s through a young man on fire for God. After spending his formative years in Europe, Andrew Murray returned to South Africa, where he became a champion for missions, led nationwide revivals, founded Christian universities, and wrote more than two hundred books and tracts on how to live the victorious Christian life.

Chapter Six

ON LOVE

Love Makes All the Difference

by Charles R. Swindoll

The first time I saw him, he was wearing knickers and knee socks. It was the late 1960s. As I listened to this man with a white goatee and a funny, screeching kind of voice, I thought, *What kind of guy is this?*

It didn't take me long to realize this man had an incredible mind. And even more—an enormous heart. Francis Schaeffer could talk on any topic and bring it back to God. Schaeffer could use any subject—philosophy, politics, art, architecture—and win another hearing from those who were trying to figure out what life was all about. Amazing. We loved him most of all not for his intellect or even his faith, though it was the pulsating power of his life, but for his courage. Whether he was before a gathering at Harvard or Berkeley, a room full of cynics and critics, or a crowded street meeting, the man stood, if necessary, all alone.

Of the long list of his books that made their way to the best-seller list, one of his best, in my opinion, is *The Mark of the Christian*. This little volume talks about our badge as believers. It's not a bumper sticker or a secret symbol like a fish or some Greek term that we put on the trunks of our cars or etch on the covers of our Bibles. The mark of the Christian is *love*.

This most unusual man caught the world's attention by his own love for people. His home in the Swiss Alps became one of the most popular places of refuge for young, confused men and women who had lost their way. These people needed a place to repair, to be accepted, to ask questions that were considered off-the-wall, inappropriate, even scandalous in their day. The Schaeffers took them in. As one man told me, "[Francis Schaeffer] loved me back to dignity and life."

Love—this is the mark of the Christian.

No one demonstrated this mark more than Jesus Himself. His love wasn't fickle. He wasn't big on it when His twelve obeyed and then weak on it when they rebelled. He was *consistently* a lover of His own.

Nowhere do we see Jesus's love more clearly than we do in John's gospel. A poignant scene from chapter 13 comes to mind. The smell of death hung in the air. The beginning of the first verse tells us that Jesus knew "His hour had come." And then comes the wonderful ending of that same verse, "Having loved His own who were in the world, He loved them to the end." This doesn't merely mean that Jesus loved them to the end of His life but that He loved them to the uttermost degree of which He was capable. We might say, He loved them "to the max." He loved them all the way—absolutely, unconditionally, and without reservation.

What security that must have given Thomas, who would later doubt. How encouraging it must have been for Peter, who would later openly deny Him.

Jesus said to the disciples after He washed their feet, "A new commandment I give to you, that you love one another, *even as I have loved you*" (13:34, emphasis added). This is a love based on the example that Jesus set during His time on earth, a love for people that sacrifices for their benefit. It's a lot easier to love God (an old commandment), whom we cannot see, than to love someone whom we live with and see at his or her very worst . . . all the while knowing he or she sees us the same way. Loving as Jesus loved (the new commandment) was to be the mark of the disciples' lives and all believers thereafter. Jesus said, "By this all men will know that you are My disciples, if you have love for one another" (13:35).

I'll let the very respected Francis Schaffer continue from here in this excerpt from his book, *The Mark of the Christian.* I encourage each of us to let this truth filter down through all the details of our lives until we, too, bear the mark of love.

The Mark of the Christian

by Francis A. Schaeffer

Through the centuries men have displayed many different symbols to show that they are Christians. They have worn marks in the lapels of their coats, hung chains about their necks, even had special haircuts.

Of course, there is nothing wrong with any of this, if one feels it is his calling. But there is a much better sign—a mark that has not been thought up just as a matter of expediency for use on some special occasion or in some specific era. It is a universal mark that is to last through all the ages of the church till Jesus comes back.

What is this mark?

At the close of his ministry, Jesus looks forward to his death on the cross, the open tomb and the ascension. Knowing that he is about to leave, Jesus prepares his disciples for what is to come. It is here that he makes clear what will be the distinguishing mark of the Christian:

> "My children, I will be with you only a little longer.
> You will look for me, and just as I told the Jews, so I
> tell you now: Where I am going, you cannot come.
> A new command I give you: Love one another. As
> I have loved you, so you must love one another. By
> this all men will know that you are my disciples, if
> you love one another." (John 13:33–35)

This passage reveals the mark that Jesus gives to label a Christian not just in one era or in one locality but at all times and all places until Jesus returns.

Notice that what he says here is not a description of a fact. It is a command which includes a condition: "A new command I give you: Love one another. As I have loved you, so you must love one another. By this all men will know that you are my disciples, *if* you love one another." An *if* is involved. If you obey, you will wear the badge Christ gave. But since this is a command, it can be violated.

The point is that it is possible to be a Christian without showing the mark, but if we expect non-Christians to know that we are Christians, we must show the mark. . . .

This is the whole point: The world is going to judge whether Jesus has been sent by the Father on the basis of something that is open to observation.

True Oneness

In John 13 and 17, Jesus talks about a real seeable oneness, a practicing oneness, a practical oneness across all lines, among all true Christians.

The Christian really has a double task. He has to practice both God's holiness and God's love. The Christian is to exhibit that God exists as the infinite-personal God; and then he is to exhibit simultaneously God's character of holiness and love. Not his holiness without his love: that is only harshness. Not his love without his holiness: that is only compromise. Anything that an individual Christian or Christian group does that fails to show the simultaneous balance of the holiness of God and the love of God presents to a watching world not a demonstration of the God who exists but a caricature of the God who exists.

According to the Scripture and the teaching of Christ, the love that is shown is to be exceedingly strong. It is not just something you mention in words once in a while.

Visible Love

What, then, does this love mean? How can it be made visible?

First, it means a very simple thing: It means that when I have made a mistake and when I have failed to love my Christian brother, I go to him and say, "I'm sorry." That is first.

It may seem a letdown—that the first thing we speak of should be so simple! But if you think it is easy, you have never tried to practice it.

In our own groups, in our own close Christian communities, even in our families, when we have shown lack of love toward another, we as Christians do not just automatically go and say we are sorry. On even the very simplest level it is never very easy.

It may sound simplistic to start with saying we are sorry and asking forgiveness, but it is not. This is the way of renewed fellowship, whether it is between a husband and wife, a parent and child, within a Christian community, or between groups. When we have shown a lack of love toward the other, we are called by God to go and say, "I'm sorry . . . I really am sorry."

If I am not willing to say, "I'm sorry," when I have wronged somebody else—especially when I have not loved him—I have not even started to think about the meaning of a Christian oneness which the world can see. The world has a right to question whether I am a Christian. And more than that, let me say it again, if I am not willing to do this very simple thing, the world has a right to question whether Jesus was sent from God and whether Christianity is true. . . .

I have observed one thing *among true Christians* in their differences in many countries: What divides and severs true Christian groups and Christians—what leaves a bitterness that can last for 20, 30 or 40 years (or for 50 or 60 years in a son's memory)—is not the issue of doctrine or belief which caused the differences in the first place. Invariably it is lack of love—and the bitter things that are said by true Christians in the midst of differences. These stick in the mind like glue. And after time passes and the differences between the Christians or the groups appear less than they did, there are still those bitter, bitter things we said in the midst of what we thought was a good and sufficient objective discussion. It is these things—these unloving attitudes and words—that cause the stench that the world can smell in the church of Jesus Christ among those who are really true Christians.

If, when we feel we must disagree as true Christians, we could simply guard our tongues and speak in love, in five or ten years the bitterness could be gone. Instead of that, we leave scars—a curse for generations. Not just a curse in the church, but a curse in the world. Newspaper headlines bear it in our Christian press, and it boils over into the secular press at times—Christians saying such bitter things about other Christians.

The world looks, shrugs its shoulders and turns away. It has not seen even the beginning of a living church in the midst of a dying culture. It has not seen the beginning of what Jesus indicates is the final apologetic—observable oneness among true Christians who are truly brothers in Christ. Our sharp tongues, the lack of love between us—not the necessary statements of differences that may exist between true Christians—these are what properly trouble the world.

How different this is from the straightforward and direct command of Jesus Christ—to show an observable oneness which may be seen by a watching world!

Forgiveness

But there is more to observable love than saying we are sorry.

There must also be open forgiveness. And though it's hard to say, "I'm sorry," it's even harder to forgive. The Bible, however, makes plain that the world must observe a forgiving spirit in the midst of God's people.

In the Lord's prayer, Jesus himself teaches us to pray, "Forgive us our trespasses, as we forgive those who trespass against us." Now this prayer, we must say quickly, is not for salvation. It has nothing to do with being born again, for we are born again on the basis of the finished work of Christ plus nothing. But it does have to do with a Christian's existential, moment-by-moment experiential relationship to God. We need a once-for-all forgiveness at justification, and we need a moment-by-moment forgiveness for our sins on the basis of Christ's work in order to be in open fellowship with God. What the Lord has taught us to pray in the Lord's prayer should make a Christian very sober every day of his life: We are asking the Lord to open to us the experiential realities of fellowship with himself as we forgive others.

Some Christians say that the Lord's prayer is not for this present era, but most of us would say it is. And yet at the same time we hardly think once in a year about our lack of a forgiving heart in relationship to God's forgiving us. Many Christians rarely or never seem to connect their own lack of reality of fellowship with God with their lack of forgiveness to men, even though they may say the Lord's prayer in a formal way over and over in their weekly Sunday worship services.

We must all continually acknowledge that we do not practice the forgiving heart as we should. And yet the prayer is "Forgive us our debts, our trespasses, as we forgive our debtors." We are to have a forgiving spirit even before the other person expresses regret for his wrong. The Lord's prayer does not suggest that when the other man is sorry, then we are to show a oneness by having a forgiving spirit. Rather, we are called upon to have a forgiving spirit without the other man having made the first step. We may still say that he is wrong, but in the midst of saying that he is wrong, we must be forgiving. . . .

Such a forgiving spirit registers an attitude of love toward others. But, even though one can call this an attitude, true forgiveness is observable. Believe me, you can look on a man's face and know where he is as far as forgiveness is concerned. And the world is called on to look upon us and see whether we have love across the groups, love across party lines. Do they observe that we say, "I'm sorry," and do they observe a forgiving heart? Let me repeat: Our love will not be perfect, but it must be substantial enough for the world to be able to observe or it does not fit into the structure of the verses in John 13 and 17. And if the world does not observe this among true Christians, the world has a right to make the two awful judgments which these verses indicate: That we are not Christians and that Christ was not sent by the Father. . . .

Francis A. Schaeffer

(1912–1984)

With his brilliant philosophical mind and his heart for those struggling with philosophical issues, Presbyterian pastor Francis Schaeffer became one of the most influential thinkers of the twentieth century. He and his wife, Edith, established a ministry base called L'Abri (French for "shelter") in the Swiss Alps, where they opened their lives to people, often the disenfranchised, who needed help finding God. Schaeffer also lectured in universities around the world and wrote more than twenty-two books.

Chapter Seven

ON SERVANTHOOD

A Challenge to Improve Your Serve

by Charles R. Swindoll

The art of unselfish living is practiced by few and mastered by even less. In today's me-first world, we shouldn't be surprised. It's difficult to cultivate a servant's heart when you are trying to survive in a dog-eat-dog society dominated by selfish pursuits. And the greatest tragedy of such an existence is what it spawns: an ultra-independent, self-sufficient, me-first mentality.

Christ-followers are called to be different. Jesus expected each of us to shine the light of God's love within this dark, lost world. We are called to serve others in our homes, schools, work places, and in every other area of our lives. That means moving beyond theory and wishful thinking and reaching out, taking risks, and doing what Scripture commands.

Jesus said, "He who has My commandments and keeps them is the one who loves Me; and he who loves Me will be loved by My Father, and I will love him and disclose Myself to him" (John 14:21). Surely that's a promise worthy to be claimed. To be loved by God and to experience the presence of Christ manifested in our lives is to discover the kingdom of heaven on earth. And because God has loved us and we love Him, we obey what Jesus taught us through His Word. We are commanded to love one another in word and in deed.

No selfless act is so small, no good deed so insignificant, that God cannot see and approve. After all, what we do as servants is not for human eyes. Furthermore, it is not for our own glory. Scripture clearly states that our service is for God's glory. God has given us the incredible honor of being His stewards who carry out the work of Jesus Christ through faithful service—among our neighborhoods and around the world.

It is, in fact, the very substance and context of the Great Commission which tells us that we are to transmit the gospel to others, not only by confessing Christ but by displaying in our lives a daily example of Christ's love.

Jesus went a step further and said that our acts of service have a deeper meaning as well. The service we offer to other people is actually evidence of our commitment to Christ. Remember? "To the extent that you did it to one of these brothers of Mine, even the least of them, you did it to Me" (Matthew 25:40).

Every act of service demonstrates our love for Christ and our obedience to Him. That's what faithful servanthood must be. Jesus said, "Whoever in the name of a disciple gives to one of these little ones even a cup of cold water to drink, truly I say to you, he shall not lose his reward" (10:42). To cherish a little child, to care for an aging parent, to speak a gentle word to a struggling neighbor or friend, to carry an armload of groceries to the car for a stranger: these, too, are demonstrations of Christ's love.

J. Oswald Sanders wrote a wonderful book back in 1967 called *Spiritual Leadership: Principles of Excellence for Every Believer*. I've about worn out my second copy. In this book, he does a masterful job detailing what he calls "the Master's Master Principle"—what we've just been talking about—servanthood. Let's get to it.

The Master's Master Principle

from *Spiritual Leadership*

by J. Oswald Sanders

Whoever wishes to become great among you

shall be your servant; and whoever wishes to be

first among you shall be slave of all.

Mark 10:43–44

In the light of the tremendous stress laid upon the leadership role in both secular and religious worlds, it is surprising to discover that in the King James Version of the Bible, for example, the term "leader" occurs only six times, three times in the singular and three in the plural. That is not to say that the theme is not prominent in the Bible, but it is usually referred to in different terms, the most prominent being "servant." It is not "Moses; my leader," but "Moses, my servant." That emphasis is consonant with Christ's teaching on the subject.[1]

Although Jesus was not a revolutionary in the political sense, many of His teachings were startling and revolutionary, and none more so than those on leadership. In the contemporary world, the term *servant* has a very lowly connotation, but that was not so as Jesus used it. Indeed, He elevated it, equating it with greatness, and that was certainly a revolutionary concept. Most of us would have no objection to being masters, but servanthood holds little attraction.

Christ's view of His kingdom was that of a community of members serving one another — *mutual service*. Paul advocates the same idea: "Through love serve one another" (Gal. 5:13). And of course our loving service is to spread to the needy world around us. But in the life of the church today, it is usually the few who serve the many.

77

Jesus well knew that such an other-worldly concept would not be welcomed by a self-pleasing world of men. But nothing less than that was what he required of those who desired to rise to leadership in His kingdom.

The contrast between the world's idea of leadership and that of Christ is brought into sharp focus in Mark 10:42–43: "You know that those who are recognized as rulers of the Gentiles lord it over them; and their great men exercise authority over them. *But it is not [to be] so among you.* But whoever wishes to become great among you shall be your servant; and whoever wishes to be first among you shall be slave of all" (italics added).

It was a lesson James and John had not mastered. They had, however, taken seriously the Master's promise "Truly I say to you, that you who have followed Me, in the regeneration when the Son of Man will sit on His glorious throne, you also shall sit upon twelve thrones, judging the twelve tribes of Israel" (Matt. 19:28). In selfish ambition they used their doting mother in an endeavor to forestall their colleagues and preempt the prime positions in the coming kingdom.

But Jesus would have none of it. There must be no lobbying for office. "You do not know what you are asking for," was the reply. Nor did they. They wanted the glory, but not the shame; the crown, but not the cross; to be masters, not servants.

Their request afforded Jesus the occasion to present two leadership principles of permanent relevance.

- *There is a sovereignty in spiritual leadership.*

"To sit on My right [hand] or on My left, this is not Mine to give; but it is for *those for whom it has been prepared*" (Mark 10:40, italics added).

Our emphasis would probably have been, "It is for those who have prepared themselves for it." But Jesus emphasized the fundamental difference in leadership principles. "It is not so among you." Places of spiritual ministry and leadership are sovereignly assigned by God. The *Good News Bible* translation of verse 40 is: "It is God who will give these places to those for whom He has prepared them."

No theological training or leadership course will automatically confer spiritual leadership or qualify one for an effective ministry. Jesus was later to tell them, "You did not choose Me, but I chose you, and appointed you" (John 15:16). To be able to affirm, "I am not here by selection of a man or the election of a group, but by the sovereign appointment of God," gives great confidence to the Christian worker.

- *There is suffering involved in spiritual leadership.*

"Are you able to drink the cup that I drink, or to be baptized with the baptism with which I am baptized?" (Mark 10:38).

Jesus was too straightforward and honest to conceal the cost in the service of the kingdom. For the fulfillment of the stupendous task entrusted to Him, He needed men and women of quality with eyes wide open, who would follow Him to the death.

To the Lord's probing question, they returned the glib answer "We are able"—thus betraying a tragic lack of self-knowledge. Jesus told them that they would indeed drink the cup and experience the baptism. They must learn that for an influential spiritual ministry there would be a steep price to pay—and that it cannot be paid in a lump sum. In the end, it cost James his head, and John finished his days in a concentration camp.

They desired to attain leadership "on the cheap," but Jesus' words soon disillusioned them. The fundamental lessons that *greatness comes only by way of servanthood*, and that first place in leadership is gained only by becoming *everybody's slave*, must have come as a great and unwelcome shock.

It is noteworthy that only once did Jesus say that He was leaving His disciples an example, and that was when He washed their feet (John 13:15)—an example of *servanthood*. And only once did any other writer say that He had left an example—and that was an example of suffering (1 Pet. 2:21). Thus the thoughts of suffering and servanthood are linked, even as they were in the life of the Lord. And is the servant greater than his Lord?

In stating that primacy in leadership comes by way of primacy in servanthood, Jesus did not have in mind mere *acts of service*, for those can be performed from very dubious motives. He meant the *spirit of servanthood*, which He expressed when He claimed, "I am among you as He that serves."

Isaiah 42:1–5, a Messianic passage, reveals what the spirit of servanthood means, and outlines in this prophetic foreview the features that would qualify the coming Messiah as the ideal Servant of the Lord.

Israel had been chosen by God to be His servant through whom He could reveal Himself to the world. But the nation failed Him dismally at every turn. However, where Israel failed, Jesus succeeded gloriously, and the principles of His life must be the pattern for ours.

Here are some of those principles:

Dependence

"Behold My Servant whom I uphold" (v. 1), a statement with Messianic significance. In fulfilling this prophetic intimation, Jesus voluntarily "emptied Himself" (Phil. 2:7), surrendering His privileges and the independent exercise of His will. Though possessing all the powers and prerogatives of deity, He voluntarily became dependent upon His Father. Though He upheld "all things by the word of His power" (Heb. 1:3), so fully did He identify Himself with the sinless infirmities of our humanity, that in His manhood He Himself needed to be upheld. That divine paradox is one of the staggering aspects of Christ's condescension. In the measure in which we adopt the same attitude will the Holy Spirit be able to use us.

Approval

"My chosen one in whom My soul delights" (v. 1). The delight of Jehovah in His ideal Servant was warmly reciprocated, for in another

Messianic reference the Son says, "I delight to do Thy will, O my God" (Psalm 40:8).

Modesty

"He will not cry out or raise His voice, nor make His voice heard in the street" (v. 2). The ministry of God's Servant would not be strident and flamboyant, but modest and self-effacing. In this day of blatant and arrogant self-advertisement, that is a most desirable quality.

The devil tempted Jesus on that point when he challenged Him to create a stir by making a miraculous leap from the parapet of the Temple. But He did not fall to the tempter's wile.

God's Servant works so quietly and unobtrusively that many even doubt His existence. His method justifies the statement "Thou art a God who hides Himself" (Isa. 45:15). It is recorded of the cherubim, those angelic servants of the Lord, that they used four of their six wings to conceal their faces and their feet—a graphic representation of contentment with hidden service (Isa. 6:2).

Empathy

"A bruised reed He will not break, and a dimly burning wick He will not extinguish" (v. 3). The Lord's Servant would be sympathetic and understanding with the weak and erring. Failing men and women are often crushed under the callous tread of their fellowmen; but not so with the ideal Servant. He was to specialize in mending bruised reeds and fanning the smoking wick into a flame.

Many, even Christian workers, ignore those who have failed and "pass by on the other side." They want a ministry more rewarding and more worthy of their powers—something more spectacular than bearing with the relapses and backslidings of frail humanity; but it is a noble work to reclaim those whom the world despises. How dimly Peter's wick burned in the judgment hall, but what a brilliant flame blazed on the day of Pentecost! His interview with God's ideal Servant put everything right.

Optimism

"He will not be disheartened or crushed, until He has established justice in the earth" (v. 4). God's Servant would be undiscourageable. A pessimist never makes an inspiring leader. Hope and optimism are essential qualities for the servant of God as he battles with the powers of darkness for the souls of men. God's Servant would be optimistic until His full objective is attained.

Anointing

"I have put My Spirit upon Him" (v. 1). By themselves, the preceding five qualities would be insufficient for His tremendous task. A touch of the supernatural was required, and that was supplied in the anointing of the Spirit. "You know of Jesus of Nazareth, how God anointed Him with the Holy Spirit and with power, and how He went about doing good" (Acts 10:38).

The same anointing that God's ideal Servant received is available for us. Until the Spirit descended upon Him at His baptism, Jesus created no stir in Nazareth, but then events of world-shaking importance began to happen. Is the servant greater than his lord? Can we dispense with that which was the prime essential for the effectiveness of His ministry on earth?

J. (John) Oswald Sanders

(1902–1992)

Hailing from the land down under, J. Oswald Sanders was God's man of influence in New Zealand. Gifted with administrative skills and a keen ability to listen and discern root issues, Sanders originally pursued a career in law but left his practice to serve in leadership of Bible colleges and mission organizations, eventually becoming the director of China Inland Fellowship. He wrote more than forty books on the Christian life with a specific bent toward Christian leadership.

Chapter Eight

ON DISCOURAGEMENT

Dealing with Discouragement

by Charles R. Swindoll

If you have known the joy of being used by God in any realm of ministry, then you have also known what it's like to be discouraged. Maybe you're there today—right now. Believe me; I understand those lonely, desperate, barren places.

One of my favorite chapters in one of my favorite books is "The Minister's Fainting Fits" in *Lectures to My Students* by Charles Haddon Spurgeon. In this chapter, he admitted to suffering through bouts of depression. He admitted to not always being vigorous and wise and ready—and to not always being courageous and happy. In fact, he even declared:

> *Before any great achievement*, some measure of . . .
> depression is very usual. . . . Such was my experience
> when I first became a pastor in London. My success
> appalled me; and the thought of the career which
> it seemed to open up, so far from elating me, cast
> me into the lowest depth, out of which I uttered my
> *miserere* and found no room for a *gloria in excelsis*.
> Who was I that I should continue to lead so great a
> multitude? I would betake me to my village obscu-
> rity, or emigrate to America, and find a solitary nest
> in the backwoods, where I might be sufficient for
> the things which would be demanded of me. . . .
> This depression comes over me whenever the Lord is
> preparing a larger blessing for my ministry.[1]

(You'll read more of Spurgeon's perspective in the excerpt that follows.)

I'll admit to you that there have been days I have identified with Spurgeon. Although maybe not as deeply as he did, I have known a deep valley of discouragement at times—even when others would think I might be caught up in pride, of all things. I have known times when I secretly wondered, *Should I even stay at it?*

If you've asked that question or one similar, let me walk alongside you for just a moment as one who can offer first-hand perspective. (Or it may be that you've come through this kind of thing, which means you are now wonderfully fitted to understand those who go through it.)

Realize first that depression is not a sin; it is a symptom of something deeper. We never think a headache is a sin, so neither is depression. However, your response to it can be. In every case, there is a problem deeper than the depression, and God wants you to discover its root cause. Ask yourself, *Do I feel this way because I've been criticized? Is it because I feel all alone? Is it because I didn't get my own way? Is it because God did something and I didn't expect it? Is it because I feel like He's picking on me? Is it because I'm exhausted? Angry? Confused?*

God gives us insight in His Word as to what we should do when we've reached the end of our tether. When He recorded lessons from the lives of David, Jonah, Paul, Elijah, and Moses, He hung those men out for all to see. (I'm always glad that God has stopped writing Scripture—forever grateful there isn't a 1 and 2 Book of Chuck.) We all have our unguarded moments, when the heavy clouds of doom seem greater than the sun of tomorrow's dawn. The question now is yours—what will you do about it?

Just as God understood those men, He understands you. Take your burden to Him. Unload your pack. He can take it. The best part: He'll never shame you or tell on you. Your struggle and mine can remain inside our cars and in the back part of our bedrooms, out under the trees of the forest or on the sandy shoreline. God can handle it all, so let it out. Let it *all* out.

I do not want to leave the impression that with a few quick Scriptures or even many heartbroken, passionate prayers that our problems will be solved. Some problems are super-complex and convoluted. But I am saying this is where the healing will start.

So go there.

The Minister's Fainting Fits

from *Lectures to My Students*

by C. H. Spurgeon

As it is recorded that David, in the heat of battle, waxed faint, so may it be written of all the servants of the Lord. Fits of depression come over the most of us. Usually cheerful as we may be, we must at intervals be cast down. The strong are not always vigorous, the wise not always ready, the brave not always courageous, and the joyous not always happy. There may be here and there men of iron, to whom wear and tear work no perceptible detriment, but surely the rust frets even these; and as for ordinary men, the Lord knows, and makes them to know, that they are but dust. Knowing by most painful experience what deep depression of spirit means, being visited therewith at seasons by no means few or far between, I thought it might be consolatory to some of my brethren if I gave my thoughts thereon, that younger men might not fancy that some strange thing had happened to them when they became for a season possessed by melancholy; and that sadder men might know that one upon whom the sun has shone right joyously did not always walk in the light.

It is not necessary by quotations from the biographies of eminent ministers to prove that seasons of fearful prostration have fallen to the lot of most, if not all of them. The life of Luther might suffice to give a thousand instances, and he was by no means of the weaker sort. His great spirit was often in the seventh heaven of exultation, and as frequently on the borders of despair. His very death-bed was not free from tempests, and he sobbed himself into his last sleep like a great wearied child. Instead of multiplying cases, let us dwell upon the reasons why these things are permitted; why it is that the children of light sometimes walk in the thick darkness; why the heralds of the daybreak find themselves at times in tenfold night.

Is it not first that *they are men*? Being men, they are compassed with infirmity, and heirs of sorrow. Well said the wise man in the Apocrypha, Ecclus xl. 1, 2, 3, 4, 5-8, "Great travail is created for all men, and a heavy yoke on the sons of Adam, from the day that they go out of their mother's womb unto that day that they return to the mother of all things—namely, their thoughts and fear of their hearts, and their imagination of things that they wail for, and the day of death. From him that sitteth in the glorious throne, to him that sitteth beneath in the earth and ashes; from him that is clothed in blue silk, and weareth a crown, to him that is clothed in simple linen—wrath, envy, trouble, and unquietness, and fear of death and rigour, and such things come to both man and beast, but sevenfold to the ungodly." Grace guards us from much of this, but because we have not more of grace we still suffer even from ills preventible. Even under the economy of redemption it is most clear that we are to endure infirmities, otherwise there were no need of the promised Spirit to help us in them. It is of need be that we are sometimes in heaviness. Good men are promised tribulation in this world, and ministers may expect a larger share than others, that they may learn sympathy with the Lord's suffering people, and so may be fitting shepherds of an ailing flock. Disembodied spirits might have been sent to proclaim the word, but they could not have entered into the feelings of those who, being in this body, do groan, being burdened; angels might have been ordained evangelists, but their celestial attributes would have disqualified them from having compassion on the ignorant; men of marble might have been fashioned, but their impassive natures would have been a sarcasm upon our feebleness, and a mockery of our wants. Men, and men subject to human passions, the all-wise God has chosen to be his vessels of grace; hence these tears, hence these perplexities and castings down.

Moreover, *most of us are in some way or other unsound physically*. Here and there we meet with an old man who could not remember that ever he was laid aside for a day; but the great mass of us labour under some form or other of infirmity, either in body or mind. Certain bodily maladies, especially those connected with the digestive organs, the liver, and the spleen, are the fruitful fountains of despondency; and, let a man strive as he may against their influence, there will be hours and circumstances in which they will for awhile overcome him. As to mental maladies, is any man altogether sane? Are we not all a little off the balance? Some minds appear to have a gloomy tinge essential to their very individuality; of them it may be said, "Melancholy marked them for her own"; fine minds withal, and ruled by noblest principles, but yet most prone to forget the silver lining, and to remember only the cloud. Such men may sing with the old poet:

> "Our hearts are broke, our harps unstringed be,
>   Our only music's sighs and groans,
> Our songs are to the tune of *lachrymae*,
>   We're fretted all to skin and bones."
>
> Thomas Washbourne

These infirmities may be no detriment to a man's career of special usefulness; they may even have been imposed upon him by divine wisdom as necessary qualifications for his peculiar course of service. Some plants owe their medicinal qualities to the marsh in which they grow; others to the shades in which alone they flourish. There are precious fruits put forth by the moon as well as by the sun. Boats need ballast as well as sail; a drag on the carriage-wheel is no hindrance when the road runs downhill. Pain has probably in some cases developed genius; hunting out the soul which otherwise might have slept like a lion in its den. Had it not been for the broken wing, some might have lost themselves in the clouds, some even of those choice doves who now bear the olive-branch in their mouths and show the way to the ark. But where in body and mind there are predisposing causes to lowness of spirit, it is no marvel if in dark moments the heart succumbs to them; the wonder in many cases is—and if inner lives could be written, men would see it so—how some ministers keep at their work at all, and still wear a smile upon their countenances. Grace has its triumphs still, and patience has its martyrs; martyrs none the less to be honoured because the flames kindle about their spirits rather than their bodies, and their burning is unseen of human eyes. The ministries of Jeremiahs are as acceptable as those of Isaiahs, and even the sullen Jonah is a true prophet of the Lord, as Nineveh felt full well. Despise not the lame, for it is written that they take the prey; but honour those who, being faint, are yet pursuing. The tender-eyed Leah was more fruitful than the beautiful Rachel, and the griefs of Hannah were more divine than the boastings of Peninnah. "Blessed are they that mourn," said the Man of Sorrows, and let none account them otherwise when their tears are salted with grace. We have the treasure of the gospel in earthen vessels, and if there be a flaw in the vessel here and there, let none wonder.

Our work, when earnestly undertaken, lays us open to attacks in the direction of depression. Who can bear the weight of souls without sometimes sinking to the dust? Passionate longings after men's conversion, if not fully satisfied (and when are they?), consume the soul with anxiety and disappointment. To see the hopeful turn aside, the godly grow cold, professors abusing their privileges, and sinners waxing more bold in sin—are not these sights enough to crush us to the earth? The kingdom comes not as we would, the reverend name is not hallowed as we desire, and for this we must weep. How can we be otherwise than sorrowful, while men believe not our report, and the divine arm is not revealed? All mental work tends to weary and to depress, for much study is a weariness of the flesh; but ours is more than mental work—it is heart work, the labour of our inmost soul. How often, on Lord's-day evenings, do we feel as if life were completely washed out of us! After pouring out our souls over our congregations, we feel like empty earthen pitchers which a child

might break. Probably, if we were more like Paul, and watched for
souls at a nobler rate, we should know more of what it is to be eaten
up by the zeal of the Lord's house. It is our duty and our privilege
to exhaust our lives for Jesus. We are not to be living specimens
of men in fine preservation, but living *sacrifices*, whose lot is to be
consumed; we are to spend and to be spent, not to lay ourselves up
in lavender, and nurse our flesh. Such soul-travail as that of a faithful
minister will bring on occasional seasons of exhaustion, when heart
and flesh will fail. Moses' hands grew heavy in intercession, and Paul
cried out, "Who is sufficient for these things?" Even John the Baptist
is thought to have had his fainting fits, and the apostles were once
amazed, and were sore afraid.

Our position in the church will also conduce to this. A minister fully
equipped for his work will usually be a spirit by himself, above,
beyond, and apart from others. The most loving of his people cannot
enter into his peculiar thoughts, cares, and temptations. In the ranks,
men walk shoulder to shoulder, with many comrades, but as the
officer rises in rank, men of his standing are fewer in number. There
are many soldiers, few captains, fewer colonels, but only one com-
mander-in-chief. So, in our churches, the man whom the Lord raises
as a leader becomes, in the same degree in which he is a superior
man, a solitary man. The mountain-tops stand solemnly apart, and
talk only with God as He visits their terrible solitudes. Men of God
who rise above their fellows into nearer communion with heavenly
things, in their weaker moments feel the lack of human sympathy.
Like their Lord in Gethsemane, they look in vain for comfort to
the disciples sleeping around them; they are shocked at the apa-
thy of their little band of brethren, and return to their secret agony
with all the heavier burden pressing upon them, because they have
found their dearest companions slumbering. No one knows, but he
who has endured it, the solitude of a soul which has outstripped
its fellows in zeal for the Lord of hosts: it dares not reveal itself, lest
men count it mad; it cannot conceal itself, for a fire burns within its
bones: only before the Lord does it find rest. Our Lord's sending out

his disciples by two and two manifested that he knew what was in men; but for such a man as Paul, it seems to me that no helpmeet was found; Barnabas, or Silas, or Luke, were hills too low to hold high converse with such a Himalayan summit as the apostle of the Gentiles. This loneliness, which if I mistake not is felt by many of my brethren, is a fertile source of depression; and our ministers' fraternal meetings, and the cultivation of holy intercourse with kindred minds will, with God's blessing, help us greatly to escape the snare.

There can be little doubt that *sedentary habits* have a tendency to create despondency in some constitutions. Burton, in his *Anatomy of Melancholy*, has a chapter upon this cause of sadness; and, quoting from one of the myriad authors whom he lays under contribution, he says— "Students are negligent of their bodies. Other men look to their tools; a painter will wash his pencils; a smith will look to his hammer, anvil, forge; a husbandman will mend his plough-irons, and grind his hatchet if it be dull; a falconer or huntsman will have an especial care of his hawks, hounds, horses, dogs, etc.; a musician will string and unstring his lute; only scholars neglect that instrument (their brain and spirits I mean) which they daily use. Well saith Lucan, 'See thou twist not the rope so hard that it break.'" To sit long in one posture, poring over a book, or driving a quill, is in itself a taxing of nature; but add to this a badly ventilated chamber, a body which has long been without muscular exercise, and a heart burdened with many cares, and we have all the elements for preparing a seething cauldron of despair, especially in the dim months of fog:

> "When a blanket wraps the day,
> When the rotten woodland drips,
> And the leaf is stamped in clay."

Let a man be naturally as blithe as a bird, he will hardly be able to bear up year after year against such a suicidal process; he will make his study a prison and his books the warders of a gaol, while nature lies outside his window calling him to health and beckoning him to joy. He who forgets the humming of the bees among the heather, the cooing of the wood-pigeons in the forest, the song of birds in the woods, the rippling of rills among the rushes, and the sighing of the wind among the pines, needs not wonder if his heart forgets to sing and his soul grows heavy. A day's breathing of fresh air upon the hills, or a few hours' ramble in the beech woods' umbrageous calm, would sweep the cobwebs out of the brain of scores of our toiling ministers who are now but half alive. A mouthful of sea air, or a stiff walk in the wind's face, would not give grace to the soul, but it would yield oxygen to the body, which is next best.

> "Heaviest the heart is in a heavy air,
> Ev'ry wind that rises blows away despair."

The ferns and the rabbits, the streams and the trouts, the fir trees and the squirrels, the primroses and the violets, the farm-yard, the new-mown hay, and the fragrant hops—these are the best medicine for hypochondriacs, the surest tonics for the declining, the best refreshments for the weary. For lack of opportunity, or inclination, these great remedies are neglected, and the student becomes a self-immolated victim.

The times most favourable to fits of depression, so far as I have experienced, may be summed up in a brief catalogue. First among them I must mention *the hour of great success*. When at last a long-cherished desire is fulfilled, when God has been glorified greatly by our means, and a great triumph achieved, then we are apt to faint. It might be imagined that amid special favours our soul would soar to heights of ecstacy, and rejoice with joy unspeakable, but it is generally the reverse. The Lord seldom exposes His warriors to the perils of exultation over victory; he knows that few of them can endure such a test, and therefore dashes their cup with bitterness. See Elias after the fire has fallen from heaven, after Baal's priests have been slaughtered and the rain has deluged the barren land! For him no notes of self-complacent music, no strutting like a conqueror in robes of triumph; he flees from Jezebel, and feeling the revulsion of his intense excitement, he prays that he may die. He who must never see death, yearns after the rest of the grave, even as Caesar, the world's monarch, in his moments of pain cried like a sick girl. Poor human nature cannot bear such strains as heavenly triumphs bring to it; there must come a reaction. Excess of joy or excitement must be paid for by subsequent depressions. While the trial lasts, the strength is equal to the emergency; but when it is over, natural weakness claims the right to show itself. Secretly sustained, Jacob can wrestle all night, but he must limp in the morning when the contest is over, lest he boast himself beyond measure. Paul may be caught up to the third heaven, and hear unspeakable things, but a thorn in the flesh, a messenger of Satan to buffet him, must be the inevitable sequel. Men cannot bear unalloyed happiness; even good men are not yet fit to have "their brows with laurel and with myrtle bound," without enduring secret humiliation to keep them in their proper place. Whirled from off our feet by a revival, carried aloft by popularity, exalted by success in soul-winning, we should be as the chaff which the wind driveth away, were it not that the gracious discipline of mercy breaks the ships of our vain glory with a strong east wind, and casts us shipwrecked, naked and forlorn, upon the Rock of Ages. . . .

To the lot of the few does it fall to pass through such a horror of great darkness as that which fell upon me after the deplorable accident at the Surrey Music Hall. I was pressed beyond measure and out of bounds with an enormous weight of misery. The tumult, the panic, the deaths, were day and night before me, and made life a burden. Then I sang in my sorrow:

> "The tumult of my thoughts
> Doth but increase my woe,
> My spirit languisheth, my heart
> Is desolate and low."

From that dream of horror I was awakened in a moment by the gracious application to my soul of the text, "Him hath God the Father exalted." The fact that Jesus is still great, let His servants suffer as they may, piloted me back to calm reason and peace. Should so terrible a calamity overtake any of my brethren, let them both patiently hope and quietly wait for the salvation of God.

.

When troubles multiply, and discouragements follow each other in long succession, like Job's messengers, then, too, amid the perturbation of soul occasioned by evil tidings, despondency despoils the heart of all its peace. Constant dropping wears away stones, and the bravest minds feel the fret of repeated afflictions. If a scanty cupboard is rendered a severer trial by the sickness of a wife or the loss of a child, and if ungenerous remarks of hearers are followed by the opposition of deacons and the coolness of members, then, like Jacob, we are apt to cry, "All these things are against me." When David returned to Ziklag and found the city burned, goods stolen, wives carried off, and his troops ready to stone him, we read, "he encouraged himself in his God"; and well was it for him that he could do so, for he would then have fainted if he had not believed to see the goodness of the Lord in the land of the living. Accumulated distresses increase each other's weight; they play into each other's hands, and, like bands of robbers, ruthlessly destroy our comfort. Wave upon wave is severe work for the strongest swimmer. The place where two seas meet strains the most seaworthy keel. If there were a regulated pause between the buffetings of adversity, the spirit would stand prepared; but when they come suddenly and heavily, like the battering of great hailstones, the pilgrim may well be amazed. The last ounce breaks the camel's back, and when that last ounce is laid upon us, what wonder if we for awhile are ready to give up the ghost!

This evil will also come upon us, we know not why, and then it is all the more difficult to drive it away. Causeless depression is not to be reasoned with, nor can David's harp charm it away by sweet discoursings. As well fight with the mist as with this shapeless, undefinable, yet all-beclouding hopelessness. One affords himself no pity when in this case, because it seems so unreasonable, and even sinful, to be troubled without manifest cause; and yet troubled the man is, even in the very depths of his spirit. If those who laugh at such melancholy did but feel the grief of it for one hour, their laughter would be sobered into compassion. Resolution might, perhaps, shake it off, but where are we to find the resolution when the whole man is unstrung? The physician and the divine may unite their skill in such cases, and both find their hands full, and more than full. The iron bolt which so mysteriously fastens the door of hope and holds our spirits in gloomy prison, needs a heavenly hand to push it back; and when that hand is seen we cry with the apostle, "Blessed be God, even the Father of our Lord Jesus Christ, the Father of mercies, and the God of all comfort; who comforteth us in all our tribulation, that we may be able to comfort them which are in any trouble, by the comfort wherewith we ourselves are comforted of God" 2 Cor. 1:3, 4. It is the God of all consolation who can:

> "With sweet oblivious antidote
> Cleanse our poor bosoms of that perilous stuff
> Which weighs upon the heart."

Simon sinks till Jesus takes him by the hand. The devil within rends and tears the poor child till the word of authority commands him to come out of him. When we are ridden with horrible fears, and weighed down with an intolerable incubus, we need but the Sun of Righteousness to rise, and the evils generated of our darkness are driven away; but nothing short of this will chase away the nightmare of the soul. . . .

C. H. (Charles Haddon) Spurgeon

(1834–1892)

Charles Spurgeon was the quintessential pastor of the nineteenth century. A Victorian-era British orator, Spurgeon is estimated to have preached to ten million people in his lifetime, most often from his London pulpit at The Metropolitan Tabernacle. Spurgeon broke from formal (and often distant and vague) preaching, adopting a more "street-friendly" rhetoric that appealed to the common person. Spurgeon's commitment to accurate, practical, and clear Bible exposition remained steadfast through his long preaching ministry.

Chapter Nine

ON FINISHING WELL

The Priceless Value of Staying the Course

by Charles R. Swindoll

Not enough is said or written today about finishing well.

A tremendous amount of material is available on motivation to get started. But let's hear it for the opposite end for a change. Let's extol the virtues of sticking with something until it is done. Of hanging tough and not losing heart. Eugene Peterson, in his fine book, *A Long Obedience in the Same Direction: Discipleship in an Instant Society*, expressed the same concern: "There is a great market for religious experience in our world; there is little enthusiasm for the patient acquisition of virtue, little inclination to sign up for a long apprenticeship in what earlier generations of Christians called holiness."[1] As you read more from this chapter, I think you'll agree: Peterson is right on. His book has spurred my thinking on this often-overlooked and forgotten subject.

I fear our generation has come dangerously near the "I'm getting tired so let's just quit" mentality. We need encouragement to keep going, and thankfully, God always provides it. He gave me a powerful reminder of this truth through a simple account I once heard. Though perhaps fictitious, this story is something I go back to whenever I'm tempted to give up.

Ignace Jan Paderewski, the famous composer-pianist, was scheduled to perform at a great concert hall in America. Present in the prestigious audience that evening was a mother with her fidgety 9-year-old son.

As she turned to talk with friends, her son could stay seated no longer. He slipped away, strangely drawn to the ebony concert grand Steinway on the stage flooded with lights. Without much notice from the sophisticated audience, the boy stared wide-eyed at the black and white keys. He placed his trembling fingers in the right location and began to play . . . "Chopsticks." The crowd hushed as hundreds of frowning faces turned in the boy's direction. Irritated, they shouted, "Where's his mother?" "Somebody stop him!"

Backstage, the master overheard the sounds out front and put together what was happening. Quietly, he rushed onto the stage. Without one word of announcement, he slipped up behind the boy, reached around both sides, and began to improvise a counter-melody to harmonize with "Chopsticks." As the two played together, Paderewski whispered in the boy's ear: "Keep going. Don't quit, son. Keep on playing . . . don't stop . . . don't quit."

And so it is with us. We hammer away on our projects, which seem as significant as "Chopsticks" in a concert hall. About the time we are ready to give it up, along comes the Master, who leans over, reaches around us, and whispers: "Keep going. Don't stop. Don't quit. Don't give up," as He provides just the right counter melody.

Do I write today to a few weary pilgrims? Listen to the Master's whispering: "Let us not become weary in doing good, for at the proper time we will reap a harvest if we do not give up" (Galatians 6:9 NIV).

So many start the Christian life like a lightning flash—hot, fast, and dazzling. But how many people can you name who are finishing the course with sustained enthusiasm and vigor? What happens along the way that swells the ranks of quitters? I really wish I knew that answer. If I did, I'd shout warnings from the pulpit Sunday after Sunday. No, better than that—I'd stoop over and whisper the answer to all the discouraged people I meet. Before it's too late . . . before they quit and instead of mastering the *Minuet* or *Concerto in A Minor*, settle for "Chopsticks."

Discipleship: "How Will You Compete with Horses?"

from *A Long Obedience in the Same Direction: Discipleship in an Instant Society*

by Eugene H. Peterson

"If you have raced with men on foot,

and they have wearied you,

how will you compete with horses?"

Jeremiah 12:5

This world is no friend to grace. A person who makes a commitment to Jesus Christ as Lord and Savior does not find a crowd immediately forming to applaud the decision nor old friends spontaneously gathering around to offer congratulations and counsel. Ordinarily there is nothing directly hostile, but an accumulation of puzzled disapproval and agnostic indifference constitutes, nevertheless, surprisingly formidable opposition.

An old tradition sorts the difficulties we face in the life of faith into the categories of the world, flesh and devil.[1] We are, for the most part, well warned of the perils of the flesh and the wiles of the devil. Their temptations have a definable shape and maintain an historical continuity. That doesn't make them any easier to resist; it does make them easier to recognize.

The world, though, is protean: each generation has the world to deal with in a new form. *World* is an atmosphere, a mood.[2] It is nearly as hard for a sinner to recognize the world's temptations as it is for a fish to discover impurities in the water. There is a sense, a feeling, that things aren't right, that the environment is not whole, but just what it is eludes analysis. We know that the spiritual atmosphere in which we live erodes faith, dissipates hope and corrupts love, but it is hard to put our finger on what is wrong.

Tourists and Pilgrims

One aspect of *world* that I have been able to identify as harmful to Christians is the assumption that anything worthwhile can be acquired at once. We assume that if something can be done at all, it can be done quickly and efficiently. Our attention spans have been conditioned by thirty-second commercials. Our sense of reality has been flattened by thirty-page abridgments.

It is not difficult in such a world to get a person interested in the message of the gospel; it is terrifically difficult to sustain the interest. Millions of people in our culture make decisions for Christ, but there is a dreadful attrition rate. Many claim to have been born again, but the evidence for mature Christian discipleship is slim. In our kind of culture anything, even news about God, can be sold if it is packaged freshly; but when it loses its novelty, it goes on the garbage heap. There is a great market for religious experience in our world; there is little enthusiasm for the patient acquisition of virtue, little inclination to sign up for a long apprenticeship in what earlier generations of Christians called holiness.

Religion in our time has been captured by the tourist mindset. Religion is understood as a visit to an attractive site to be made when we have adequate leisure. For some it is a weekly jaunt to church. For others, occasional visits to special services. Some, with a bent for religious entertainment and sacred diversion, plan their lives around special events like retreats, rallies and conferences. We go to see a new personality, to hear a new truth, to get a new experience and so, somehow, expand our otherwise humdrum lives. The religious life is defined as the latest and the newest: Zen, faith-healing, human potential, parapsychology, successful living, choreography in the chancel, Armageddon. We'll try anything—until something else comes along.

I don't know what it has been like for pastors in other cultures and previous centuries, but I am quite sure that for a pastor in Western culture in the latter part of the twentieth century the aspect of *world* that makes the work of leading Christians in the way of faith most difficult is what Gore Vidal has analyzed as "today's passion for the immediate and the casual."[3] Everyone is in a hurry. The persons whom I lead in worship, among whom I counsel, visit, pray, preach, and teach, want short cuts. They want me to help them fill out the form that will get them instant credit (in eternity). They are impatient for results. They have adopted the lifestyle of a tourist and only want the high points. But a pastor is not a tour guide. I have no interest in telling apocryphal religious stories at and around dubiously identified sacred sites. The Christian life cannot mature under such conditions and in such ways.

Friedrich Nietzsche, who saw this area of spiritual truth, at least, with great clarity wrote, "The essential thing 'in heaven and earth' is . . . that there should be long obedience in the same direction; there thereby results, and has always resulted in the long run, something which has made life worth living."[4] It is this "long obedience in the same direction" which the mood of the world does so much to discourage.

In going against the stream of the world's ways there are two biblical designations for people of faith that are extremely useful: *disciple* and *pilgrim*. Disciple *(mathetes)* says we are people who spend our lives apprenticed to our master, Jesus Christ. We are in a growing-learning relationship, always. A disciple is a learner, but not in the academic setting of a schoolroom, rather at the work site of a craftsman. We do not acquire information about God but skills in faith.

Pilgrim (parepidemos) tells us we are people who spend our lives going someplace, going to God, and whose path for getting there is the way, Jesus Christ. We realize that "this world is not my home" and set out for the "Father's house." Abraham, who "went out," is our archetype. Jesus, answering Thomas' question, "Lord, we do not know where you are going; how can we know the way?" gives us directions: "I am the way, and the truth, and the life; no one comes to the Father, but by me" (Jn. 14:5–6). The letter to the Hebrews defines our program: "Therefore, since we are surrounded by so great a cloud of witnesses, let us lay aside every weight, and sin which clings so closely, and let us run with perseverance the race that is set before us, looking to Jesus the pioneer and perfecter of our faith" (Heb. 12:1–2).

A Dog-eared Songbook

In the pastoral work of training people in discipleship and accompanying them in pilgrimage, I have found, tucked away in the Hebrew Psalter, an old dog-eared songbook. I have used it to provide continuity in guiding others in the Christian way, and directing people of faith in the conscious and continuous effort which develops into maturity in Christ. The old songbook is called, in Hebrew, *šire hamm'elot*—the Songs of Ascents. The songs are the psalms numbered 120 through 134 in the book of Psalms.

These fifteen psalms were likely sung, possibly in sequence, by Hebrew pilgrims as they went up to Jerusalem to the great worship festivals. Jerusalem was the highest city geographically in Palestine,[5] and so all who traveled there spent much of their time ascending.[6] But the ascent was not only literal, it was also a metaphor: the trip to Jerusalem acted out a life lived upward toward God, an existence that advanced from one level to another in developing maturity. What Paul described as "the upward call of God in Christ Jesus" (Phil. 3:14).

Three times a year faithful Hebrews made that trip (Ex. 23:14–17; 34:22–24). The Hebrews were a people whose salvation had been accomplished in the exodus, whose identity had been defined at Sinai and whose preservation had been assured in the forty years of wilderness wandering. As such a people they regularly climbed the road to Jerusalem to worship. They refreshed their memories of God's saving ways at the Feast of Passover in the spring; they renewed their commitments as God's covenanted people at the Feast of Pentecost in early summer; they responded as a blessed community to the best that God had for them at the Feast of Tabernacles in the autumn. They were a redeemed people, a commanded people, a blessed people. These foundational realities were preached and taught and praised at the annual feasts. Between feasts the people lived these realities in daily discipleship until the time came to go up to the mountain city again as pilgrims to renew the covenant.

This picture of the Hebrews singing these fifteen psalms as they left their routines of discipleship and made their way from towns and villages, farms and cities, as pilgrims up to Jerusalem has become embedded in the Christian devotional imagination. It is our best background for understanding life as a faith-journey.

We know that our Lord from a very early age "went up" to Jerusalem for the annual feasts (Lk. 2:41–42). We continue to identify with the first disciples who "were on the road, going up to Jerusalem, and Jesus was walking ahead of them; and they were amazed, and those who followed were afraid" (Mk. 10:32). We also are amazed and afraid for there is wonder upon unexpected wonder on this road, and there are fearful specters to be met. Singing the fifteen psalms is a way both to express the amazing grace and to quiet the anxious fears.

There are no better "songs for the road" for those who travel the way of faith in Christ, a way that has so many continuities with the way of Israel. Since many (not all) essential items in Christian discipleship are incorporated in these songs, they provide a way to remember who we are and where we are going. I have not sought to produce scholarly expositions of these psalms but to offer practical meditations which use these tunes for stimulus, encouragement and guidance. If we learn to sing them well, they can be a kind of vade mecum for a Christian's daily walk.

Between the Times

Paul Tournier, in *A Place for You*, describes the experience of being in between — between the time we leave home and arrive at our destination; between the time we leave adolescence and arrive at adulthood; between the time we leave doubt and arrive at faith.[7] It is like the time when a trapeze artist lets go the bars and hangs in midair, ready to catch another support: it is a time of danger, of expectation, of uncertainty, of excitement, of extraordinary aliveness.

Christians will recognize how appropriately these psalms may be sung between the times: between the time we leave the world's environment and arrive at the Spirit's assembly; between the time we leave sin and arrive at holiness; between the time we leave home on Sunday morning and arrive in church with the company of God's people; between the time we leave the works of the law and arrive at justification by faith. They are songs of transition, brief hymns that provide courage, support and inner direction for getting us to where God is leading us in Jesus Christ.

Meanwhile the world whispers, "Why bother? There is plenty to enjoy without involving yourself in all that. The past is a grave-yard; ignore it; the future is a holocaust; avoid it. There is no payoff for discipleship; there is no destination for pilgrimage. Get God the quick way; buy instant charisma." But other voices speak, if not more attractively, at least more truly. Thomas Szasz, in his therapy and writing, has attempted to revive respect for what he calls the "simplest and most ancient of human truths: namely, that life is an arduous and tragic struggle; that what we call 'sanity' — what we mean by 'not being schizophrenic' — has a great deal to do with competence, earned by struggling for excellence; with compassion, hard won by confronting conflict; and with modesty and patience, acquired through silence and suffering."[8] His testimony validates the decision of those who commit themselves to explore the world of the Psalms of Ascents, who mine them for wisdom and sing them for cheerfulness.

These psalms were no doubt used in such ways by the multitudes Isaiah described as traveling "up to the mountain of the LORD, to the house of the God of Jacob; that he may teach us his ways and that we may walk in his paths" (Is. 2:3). They are also evidence of what Isaiah promised when he said, "You shall have a song as in the night when a holy feast is kept; and gladness of heart, as when one sets out to the sound of the flute to go to the mountain of the LORD, to the Rock of Israel" (Is. 30:29).

Everyone who travels the road of faith requires assistance from time to time. We need cheering up when spirits flag; we need direction when the way is unclear. . . .

For those who choose to live no longer as tourists, but as pilgrims, the Psalms of Ascents combine all the cheerfulness of a travel song, with the practicality of a guidebook and map. Their unpretentious brevity is excellently described by William Faulkner. "They are not monuments, but footprints. A monument only says, 'At least I got this far,' while a footprint says, 'This is where I was when I moved again.' "[9]

Eugene H. Peterson

(1932–)

A modern-day pastor-poet, Eugene Peterson's contribution to the spiritual lives of our generation is impossible to measure. In addition to The Message, *his fresh paraphrase of the Bible, Peterson has authored numerous books that focus on the Christian life and life in the ministry. Peterson pastored Christ Our King Presbyterian Church in Bel Air, Maryland, and served as professor of spiritual theology at Regent College in Vancouver, British Columbia. Peterson and his wife, Jan, live in "big sky country" of Montana.*

Epilogue

MAN ALIVE
TO READING

Man Alive to Reading

by Charles R. Swindoll

I want to tell you about something that I must do to survive, both professionally and personally.

I have to read.

Reading is a dying art. How illiterate this generation has become is almost scandalous. Christian publishers tell Christian writers to be sure and write for women because most men don't read. Most of the people in Christian bookstores are women. The next top category is pastors. And the least group of people are the general Christian audience . . . especially men. I think it would shock us to know how little our culture reads, even the people who do surgery on our bodies, defend us in courtrooms, write our music, entertain us on television, and preach our sermons.

If a Ph.D. doesn't continue to read in his or her field, he or she is virtually obsolete in five years. If that's true of the brightest people, think of where that leaves the rest of us. I'm thinking not only of reading within our individual realms of interest but of reading in many areas far removed from what we do for a living.

John Wesley once said to a group of young ministers, "Either read or get out of the ministry!"[1] Reading isn't a recent fad. The need to read has been with us for centuries.

Allow me to share with you many ways reading can play a part in your personal, professional, and even spiritual development. Here's the plan: first, I'll touch on the benefits I find in reading. Second, I'll share some suggestions on how to become a reader.

What Does Reading Do for Us?

For those of you who need a little motivation, let's talk about the benefits of reading. Why should we read?

Reading sweeps away our mental cobwebs. It is a fact that as we age, we plunge ever-deeper into the ruts of our routines. Certainly, some routine is essential for an organized life. Some responsibilities carry with them certain time demands, certain schedules, certain deadlines. But all these become painfully routine. Reading helps wipe away the cobwebs of our minds. It clobbers our brittle, narrow opinions with new ideas and fresh perspectives. It keeps us young and on a learning curve. I need that.

Reading broadens our minds. I get that from Francis Bacon, who said, "Reading maketh a full man, conference a ready man, and writing an exact man." [2] Reading gets us into areas in which we would not normally traffic. It does so with a sense of resourcefulness. It's not just an imaginative drift, like being on the sea without a sail. No, reading gives us a rudder into new areas, directing us there and then toward helpful destinations.

When I was in seminary, I gave blood every six weeks for one purpose: to buy books. I remember buying Keil and Delitzsch, an extensive Old Testament commentary series, with what Cynthia and I called "blood money." I would go in, give a pint of blood, and receive $20 in return. Then, I'd head over to the bookstore and pay it down on another volume. I think I built a tenth of my personal library back then with "blood money" made during my years in seminary. Later, I got anemic and couldn't give blood any more.

I had a professor in school who used to say, "If you have two thousand volumes in your library, you have two thousand profs at your fingertips!" It doesn't matter where you are—you can carry those tutors with you. They're available. All you've got to do is reach over and get their counsel. There isn't a week in my life that I do not spend time poring over a book (usually books) from my library.

Reading sharpens the edge of our perception. Reading is a discipline that enhances the power of concentration. Before I was a reader, I had a very short concentration span. Truth be told, I needed to be entertained. I didn't want to think, nor was I challenged to think. I didn't like teachers who forced me to think, and I wasn't interested in books that required me to think. I certainly wasn't interested in professions that demanded it!

I have now changed. Thankfully, I've learned that in the process of reading, my perceptions are sharpened. People who read ask better questions. People who read are less gullible. Reading gets me to push through the fog of verbosity. As a reader, I see through many of the advertising slogans that barrage me from every angle. A lot of it is phony and full of froth.

Readers also tend to have less rigid, less unchanging, less dogmatic opinions. They tolerate a broader world. But they don't lose their convictions; rather, reading helps solidify those convictions. The longer I live, the fewer things I would die for. But of those things I would die for, I'd fight for them to my last day. Reading has helped me distill my list and determine what those convictions are.

Reading makes us more interesting to be around. We have all had the same experience: boring small talk. Let's face it; after you've been through the weather, who won the game, the interest rate, and your most recent surgery, you've just about run out of subjects to talk about. How thrilling it is to be around a person who can talk outside the realm of the expected! How fun it is to have somebody come alongside and really puncture my present moment with a terrific thought that person got from something he or she read.

Because of this, reading is a tremendous tool for evangelism. If I didn't read, I don't know how I could begin to talk to a person who doesn't yet know Christ. The world of reading has opened up for me levels of conversation with people that lock us together. It's wonderful.

Before I began to read very much, my answers to people's spiritual questions were simplistic and formula oriented. Reading has helped break that down. It has helped me replace simplistic thinking with meaningful reasoning.

Reading helps us put real feelings into our lives. If you're a person who doesn't leave a lot of room for feeling, reading will help that change. I was raised to express opinions, not emotions. But when you read a book like *The View from a Hearse* or *A Severe Mercy*, you discover ways to express your grief. When I read *A Severe Mercy*, I wept at places where Vanauken didn't plan for the reader to weep, but Vanauken put his finger on an emotion that I hadn't been able to express (and needed to) for at least a decade or two. I'm now a firm believer that you don't really get over grief until you've fully expressed it. Reading will uncover other feelings too. It expands your emotional vocabulary.

Reading gives us a keener ability to glean truth from Scripture. As I grew more interested in reading, I was able to get insights from the Bible that I wouldn't have had decades before. Let me show you an example of how this transpires. Paul exhorted Timothy, the young minister-in-the-making, with reading: "Until I come, give attention to reading, to exhortation and to teaching" (1 Timothy 4:13). In the New American Standard version, "to the public reading of Scripture" was added by the editors to help make it clear. But "public" and "of Scripture" are not in the original text. It simply says, reading. Basically, Paul said to Timothy, "Be a reader. And use the reading in your exhortation and in your teaching."

Paul didn't tell Timothy something that Paul himself didn't do. Paul was in a Mamertine dungeon, in Rome no doubt. It was cold. It was dark. It was damp. He was lonely. He was facing sure death. But look at what he wrote to Timothy: "When you come, bring the cloak, bring the cloak which I left at Troas, and the books, especially the parchments" (2 Timothy 4:13). He said, "Bring the books." There he was, dying in a dungeon, and he said, "I miss my books. Bring along the books."

I find, as a reader, that words from Scripture take on deeper meaning, because I ponder them in extrabiblical reading. Mental pictures come easier to me. My imagination is quickened. The same will be true for you. I am quicker to see relationships between phrases. Again, you will have the same experience.

Jesus's words must have really rebuked the Pharisees when He said, often, "Have you not heard? Haven't you read?" They had read black print on parchment, but they hadn't really seen its relationship with truth. In other words, Jesus was saying, "Haven't you compared the truth of Scripture to this reality in principle? Haven't you ever seen—you rabbis, you teachers of the truth, you scribes who know the scrolls so well—the value of what this *means*?"

I hope that first and foremost your favorite book is the Bible. But I hope that your reading isn't limited just to Scripture. Paul was a student of the world outside his own. He cited from memory several contemporary poets (Acts 17 and Titus 1). And when close to death in a dungeon, he missed his books (2 Timothy 4:13). Paul was a well-read man.

How to Become a Reader Yourself

Have I convinced you yet? If so, allow me to offer you a few ways to get started.

Start with a book that interests you. Find a book on a subject that intrigues you, a book that comes highly recommended, or one with a style of writing that is appealing to you. Select it carefully. Take your time.

Carry a book with you to fill up the blank spaces of time. I usually have a book tucked in the door of my car. If you're eating a meal alone, bring a book along. Instead of watching television or browsing the Internet or playing a game on your smart phone, try an hour of reading. Before bed, if you have trouble going to sleep, hey, get one of my books. (It'll put you out fast, really fast.)

If you're just looking to fill your time, you don't even have to be that choosey. Get a paperback. Get one that seems intriguing enough to stretch you, and then get at it. Fill your time with a book that has some intrigue and some story and some style to it.

Discipline yourself to finish the first book before you start the next one. Some volumes you just need to scan over, rather than digest. But if you're going to start right, I recommend that you finish the first one.

Read not to contradict or confute, not to believe or take for granted, not to find talk in discourse but to weigh and consider. Some books are to be tasted. Others are to be swallowed. And a few are to be chewed slowly and digested. There will be a handful of books that should be read and re-read over the course of a lifetime.

In closing, let me give you some final thoughts, shotgun style:

- *Share what you've read.* If you write a little, add quotes from the books you've read to letters or e-mails. People appreciate hearing a line from someone else.

- *Pass on to others the gift of a book.* I don't know of a gift I like to receive or to give away more than a book. It always excites me.

- *Be sensitive to spiritual things.* As a Christian, look for bridges and insights into scriptural truths.

- *Vary your reading diet and speed.* Read widely. Read outside the realm of your interest. Read some things quickly, and read some things slowly. If you want to keep from being ultra-critical, read from the other side of an argument you feel strongly about. One of the finest ways I have learned to lead is by putting myself in the shoes of another person to see where he or she is coming from.

- *Read fiction and nonfiction.* Read fun stuff and serious stuff. Read history and biography. All of it is useful.

- *Learn new words.* Add them to your vocabulary by inserting them in conversations.

I hope that these thoughts have inspired you, encouraged you, and sparked your interest in reading. It has been a lifeline for me. And I hope it will be for you as well.

My sister, Luci, sums up beautifully what we've been talking about:

> Books are like friends . . . individual, unique, and inestimable. They each contribute something different yet valuable to our lives. They should be chosen carefully, enjoyed lovingly, and given time to grow on us. Reading brings us from darkness into light, from ignorance to knowledge, from imprisonment to freedom. By means of reading we are better able to ferret out the meanings and possibilities of life. The voices of Reason, Victory, Beauty, Faith, History, Poetry, Science . . . reach out to instruct and to encourage us from the author's pen, and we are better for it.[3]

How to Begin a Relationship with God

O f all the books in all the world, none can compare to the eternal Word of God. The Bible is a living, encouraging, enlightening map that lays out the path to knowing God. The Bible marks this path with four essential truths. Let's look at each marker in detail.

Our Spiritual Condition: Totally Depraved

The first truth is rather personal. One look in the mirror of Scripture, and our human condition becomes painfully clear:

> "There is none righteous, not even one;
> There is none who understands,
> There is none who seeks for God;
> All have turned aside, together they have become
>   useless;
> There is none who does good,
> There is not even one." (Romans 3:10–12)

We are all sinners through and through — totally depraved. Now, that doesn't mean we've committed every atrocity known to humankind. We're not as *bad* as we can be, just as *bad off* as we can be. Sin colors all our thoughts, motives, words, and actions.

If you've been around a while, you likely already believe it. Look around. Everything around us bears the smudge marks of our sinful nature. Despite our best efforts to create a perfect world, crime statistics continue to soar, divorce rates keep climbing, and families keep crumbling.

Something has gone terribly wrong in our society and in ourselves — something deadly. Contrary to how the world would repackage it, "me-first" living doesn't equal rugged individuality and freedom; it equals death. As Paul said in his letter to the Romans,

"The wages of sin is death" (Romans 6:23)—our spiritual and physical death that comes from God's righteous judgment of our sin, along with all of the emotional and practical effects of this separation that we experience on a daily basis. This brings us to the second marker: God's character.

God's Character: Infinitely Holy

How can God judge us for a sinful state we were born into? Our total depravity is only half the answer. The other half is God's infinite holiness.

The fact that we know things are not as they should be points us to a standard of goodness beyond ourselves. Our sense of injustice in life on this side of eternity implies a perfect standard of justice beyond our reality. That standard and source is God Himself. And God's standard of holiness contrasts starkly with our sinful condition.

Scripture says that "God is Light, and in Him there is no darkness at all" (1 John 1:5). God is absolutely holy—which creates a problem for us. If He is so pure, how can we who are so impure relate to Him?

Perhaps we could try being better people, try to tilt the balance in favor of our good deeds, or seek out methods for self-improvement. Throughout history, people have attempted to live up to God's standard by keeping the Ten Commandments or living by their own code of ethics. Unfortunately, no one can come close to satisfying the demands of God's law. Romans 3:20 says, "By the works of the Law no flesh will be justified in His sight; for through the Law comes the knowledge of sin."

Our Need: A Substitute

So here we are, sinners by nature and sinners by choice, trying to pull ourselves up by our own bootstraps to attain a relationship with our holy Creator. But every time we try, we fall flat on our faces. We can't live a good enough life to make up for our sin, because God's standard isn't "good enough"—it's *perfection*. And we can't make amends for the offense our sin has created without dying for it.

Who can get us out of this mess?

If someone could live perfectly, honoring God's law, and would bear sin's death penalty for us—in our place—then we would be saved from our predicament. But is there such a person? Thankfully, yes!

Meet your substitute—*Jesus Christ*. He is the One who took death's place for you!

> [God] made [Jesus Christ] who knew no sin to be sin on our behalf, so that we might become the righteousness of God in Him. (2 Corinthians 5:21)

God's Provision: A Savior

God rescued us by sending His Son, Jesus, to die on the cross for our sins (1 John 4:9–10). Jesus was fully human and fully divine (John 1:1, 18), a truth that ensures His understanding of our weaknesses, His power to forgive, and His ability to bridge the gap between God and us (Romans 5:6–11). In short, we are "justified as a gift by His grace through the redemption which is in Christ Jesus" (Romans 3:24). Two words in this verse bear further explanation: *justified* and *redemption*.

Justification is God's act of mercy, in which He declares righteous the believing sinners while we are still in our sinning state. Justification doesn't mean that God *makes* us righteous, so that we never sin again, rather that He *declares* us righteous—much like a judge pardons a guilty criminal. Because Jesus took our sin upon Himself and suffered our judgment on the cross, God forgives our debt and proclaims us PARDONED.

Redemption is Christ's act of paying the complete price to release us from sin's bondage. God sent His Son to bear His wrath for all of our sins—past, present, and future (Romans 3:24–26; 2 Corinthians 5:21). In humble obedience, Christ willingly endured the shame of the cross for our sake (Mark 10:45; Romans 5:6–8; Philippians 2:8). Christ's death satisfied God's righteous demands. He no longer holds our sins against us, because His own Son paid the penalty for them. We are freed from the slave market of sin, never to be enslaved again!

Placing Your Faith in Christ

These four truths describe how God has provided a way to Himself through Jesus Christ. Because the price has been paid in full by God, we must respond to His free gift of eternal life in total faith and confidence in Him to save us. We must step forward into the relationship with God that He has prepared for us—not by doing good works or by being a good person, but by coming to Him just as we are and accepting His justification and redemption by faith.

> For by grace you have been saved through faith;
> and that not of yourselves, it is the gift of God;
> not as a result of works, so that no one may boast.
> (Ephesians 2:8–9)

We accept God's gift of salvation simply by placing our faith in Christ alone for the forgiveness of our sins. Would you like to enter a relationship with your Creator by trusting in Christ as your Savior? If so, here's a simple prayer you can use to express your faith:

> *Dear God,*
>
> *I know that my sin has put a barrier between You and me. Thank You for sending Your Son, Jesus, to die in my place. I trust in Jesus alone to forgive my sins, and I accept His gift of eternal life. I ask Jesus to be my personal Savior and the Lord of my life. Thank You. In Jesus's name, amen.*

If you've prayed this prayer or one like it and you wish to find out more about knowing God and His plan for you in the Bible, contact us at Insight for Living. Our contact information is on the following pages.

We Are Here for You

If you desire to find out more about knowing God and His plan for you in the Bible, contact us. Insight for Living provides staff pastors who are available for free written correspondence or phone consultation. These seminary-trained and seasoned counselors have years of experience and are well-qualified guides for your spiritual journey.

Please feel welcome to contact your regional Pastoral Ministries by using the information below:

United States
Insight for Living
Pastoral Ministries
Post Office Box 269000
Plano, Texas 75026-9000
USA
972-473-5097, Monday through Friday,
8:00 a.m.–5:00 p.m. central time
www.insight.org/contactapastor

Canada
Insight for Living Canada
Pastoral Ministries
PO Box 8 Stn A
Abbotsford BC   V2T 6Z4
1-800-663-7639
info@insightforliving.ca

Australia, New Zealand, and South Pacific
Insight for Living Australia
Pastoral Care
Post Office Box 443
Boronia, VIC 3155
AUSTRALIA
1 300 467 444

United Kingdom and Europe
Insight for Living United Kingdom
Pastoral Care
PO Box 553
Dorking
RH4 9EU
UNITED KINGDOM
0800 915 9364
+44 (0)1306 640156
pastoralcare@insightforliving.org.uk

Endnotes

Chapter 1: On Pursuing One's Calling

My Defining Moment by Charles R. Swindoll

1. Jim Elliot, as quoted in Elisabeth Elliot, *Through Gates of Splendor* (Wheaton, Ill.: Tyndale, 1981), 172.

Chapter 2: On Intimacy with God

Knowing the Unknowable by Charles R. Swindoll

1. A. W. Tozer, *The Knowledge of the Holy: The Attributes of God: Their Meaning in the Christian Life* (San Francisco: HarperSanFrancisco, 1992), 9.

God Incomprehensible from *The Knowledge of the Holy* by A.W. Tozer

1. Nicholas of Cusa, *The Vision of God* (New York: E. P. Dutton & Sons, 1928), 60.

2. Nicholas of Cusa, *The Vision of God*, 58–59.

3. Richard Rolle, *The Amending of Life* (London: John M. Watkins, 1922), 83–84.

4. *The Cloud of Unknowing* (London: John M. Watkins, 1946).

5. Michael de Molinos, *The Spiritual Guide*, 6th ed. (London: Methune & Co., Ltd., 1950), 56.

6. Molinos, *The Spiritual Guide*, 56–57.

Chapter 3: On Trials and Testing

The Essential Season of Suffering by Charles R. Swindoll

1. A. W. Tozer, *The Root of the Righteous* (Camp Hill, Pa.: Christian Publications, 1986), 137.

2. C. S. Lewis, *The Problem of Pain* (New York: Macmillan, 1962), 93.

Chapter 5: On Joy

The Secret to Joyful Living by Charles R. Swindoll

1. Andrew Murray, *Abide in Christ* (Springdale, Pa.: 1979), 164.

Chapter 7: On Servanthood

The Master's Master Principle from *Spiritual Leadership*
by J. Oswald Sanders

1. Paul S. Rees, "The Community Clue," *Life of Faith*, 26 September 1976,
    p. 3.

Chapter 8: On Discouragement

Dealing with Discouragement by Charles R. Swindoll

1. C. H. Spurgeon, "The Minister's Fainting Fits," in *Lectures to My
    Students: Complete and Unabridged* (Grand Rapids: Zondervan, 1982),
    159–60.

Chapter 9: On Finishing Well

The Priceless Value of Staying the Course by Charles R. Swindoll

1. Eugene H. Peterson, *A Long Obedience in the Same Direction: Discipleship
    in an Instant Society* (Downers Grove, Ill.: InterVarsity, 1980), 12.

Discipleship: "How Will You Compete with Horses?" from
A Long Obedience in the Same Direction: Discipleship in an Instant Society
by Eugene H. Peterson

1. *The Book of Common Prayer* (New York: The Church Pension Fund,
    1945), 276.

2. Amos T. Wilder writes, "World means more than 'mankind fallen away
    from God.' . . . The world is created and loved by God, and Christ has
    come to save it. But it is ephemeral, subject to decay and death; more-
    over, it has fallen under the control of the evil one, and therefore into
    darkness." *The Interpreter's Bible*, ed. George Arthur Buttrick (Nashville:
    Abingdon, 1952), XII, 238.

3. Gore Vidal, *Matters of Fact and Fiction* (New York: Random House,
    1977), 86.

4. Friedrich Nietzsche, *Beyond Good and Evil*, trans. Helen Zimmern (London: 1907), Section 188, 106–9.

5. *Editor's Note:* Actually, the highest city in the Judean hill country is Hebron, with Jerusalem coming in second.

6. There is no independent documentation that the Psalms of Ascents were used thus, and therefore no consensus among scholars that they were associated with the pilgrimage journeys to Jerusalem. The connection is conjectural but not at all fanciful. Commentators, both Jewish and Christian, have interpreted these psalms in this framework.

7. Paul Tournier, *A Place for You* (New York: Harper & Row, 1968), 163.

8. Thomas Szasz, *Schizophrenia, The Sacred Symbol of Psychiatry* (Garden City: Doubleday, 1978), 72.

9. William Faulkner, quoted in Sam di Bonaventura's Program Notes to Elie Siegmeister's Symphony No. 5, Baltimore Symphony Concert, May 5, 1977.

Epilogue

Man Alive to Reading by Charles R. Swindoll

1. John Wesley, as quoted in Charles R. Swindoll, *Come Before Winter and Share My Hope* (Grand Rapids: Zondervan, 1983), 306.

2. Francis Bacon, as quoted in John Bartlett, *Familiar Quotations*, 13th ed. (Boston: Little, Brown, 1955), 121.

3. Luci Swindoll, *Wide My World, Narrow My Bed* (Portland, Ore.: Multnomah, 1982), 81–82.

Build Your Own Library
More Classic Books from Chuck Swindoll's Favorite Authors

Most of these books are widely available from a number of publishers and in various editions. You may also find electronic versions for sale on the Internet.

In addition to *Through Gates of Splendor* by Elisabeth Elliot, we recommend:

- *Shadow of the Almighty: The Life and Testament of Jim Elliot*
- *Let Me Be a Woman*
- *A Path Through Suffering: Discovering the Relationship between God's Mercy and Our Pain*

In addition to *The Knowledge of the Holy: The Attributes of God: Their Meaning in the Christian Life* and *The Root of the Righteous* by A.W. Tozer, we recommend:

- *The Pursuit of God: The Human Thirst for the Divine*
- *Mornings with Tozer: Daily Devotional Readings*

In addition to *The Secret of Guidance* by F. B. Meyer, we recommend:

- *Our Daily Walk*
- *The Best of F. B. Meyer: 120 Daily Devotions to Nurture Your Spirit and Refresh Your Soul*
- *The Life of Joseph: Beloved, Hated, and Exalted*

In addition to *Abide in Christ* by Andrew Murray, we recommend:

- *Absolute Surrender*
- *Humility: The Journey toward Holiness*
- *With Christ in the School of Prayer*

In addition to *The Mark of the Christian* by Francis A. Schaeffer, we recommend:

- *The God Who Is There*
- *Escape from Reason*
- *He Is There and He Is Not Silent*

In addition to *Spiritual Leadership* by J. Oswald Sanders, we recommend:

- *Spiritual Maturity: Principles of Spiritual Growth for Every Believer*
- *Spiritual Discipleship: Principles of Following Christ for Every Believer*
- *The Incomparable Christ: The Person and Work of Jesus*

In addition to *Lectures to My Students* by C. H. Spurgeon, we recommend:

- *All of Grace*
- *Morning and Evening: Daily Reading*
- *Finding Peace in Life's Storms*

In addition to *A Long Obedience in the Same Direction: Discipleship in an Instant Society* by Eugene H. Peterson, we recommend:

- *The Message: The Bible in Contemporary Language*
- *Five Smooth Stones for Pastoral Work*
- *Run with the Horses: The Quest for Life at Its Best*

Ordering Information

If you would like to order additional copies of *Meet Me in the Library: Readings from Eight Writers Who Shaped My Life* or order other Insight for Living resources, please contact the office that serves you.

United States
Insight for Living
Post Office Box 269000
Plano, Texas 75026-9000
USA
1-800-772-8888 (Monday through Friday,
7:00 a.m.–7:00 p.m. central time)
www.insight.org
www.insightworld.org

Canada
Insight for Living Canada
PO Box 8 Stn A
Abbotsford BC V2T 6Z4
1-800-663-7639
www.insightforliving.ca

Australia, New Zealand, and South Pacific
Insight for Living Australia
Post Office Box 443
Boronia, VIC 3155
AUSTRALIA
1300 467 444
www.insight.asn.au

United Kingdom and Europe
Insight for Living United Kingdom
PO Box 553
Dorking
RH4 9EU
UNITED KINGDOM
0800 915 9364
www.insightforliving.org.uk

Other International Locations
International constituents may contact the U.S. office through
our Web site (www.insightworld.org), mail queries, or by calling
+1-972-473-5136.